W9-BAN-131

Floating
Takes Faith

Floating Takes Faith

ANCIENT WISDOM FOR A MODERN WORLD

RABBI DAVID J. WOLPE

BEHRMAN HOUSE

www.behrmanhouse.com

Copyright © 2004 by David J. Wolpe

Published by Behrman House, Inc.
Springfield, NJ 07081
www.behrmanhouse.com

Designed by Howard Levy / Red Rooster Group, NY
Manufactured in the United States of America

Library of Congress Cataloging-In-Publication Data

Wolpe, David J.
Floating Takes Faith: Ancient Wisdom For A Modern World / David J. Wolpe
  p. cm
ISBN 0-87441-733-3 (hardcover)
1. Judaism. 2. Jewish way of life. 3. Spiritual life—Judaism. I. Title.

BM45.W65 2004
296.7'2—dc22

                                                                2004012571

~ For Samara ~

Contents

Preface ~ ix

The First Question ~ xi

A Remarkable People ~ 1

A Land of Promise ~ 23

God, Faith, and Doubt ~ 37

Forming Families ~ 61

Leadership and Learning ~ 75

Spiritual Growth ~ 103

Virtues and Vices ~ 135

Life, Death, and Afterlife ~ 163

Preface

JEWISH TRADITION IS NOT FAMOUS for brevity. The Talmud piles volume upon volume, commentary upon commentary. We are rich with stories, personalities, centuries. A people with such a long history has too much to tell. Jews are famously gifted with words and powerfully driven to speak and to understand.

So it was against the grain that I asked my friend Gary Rosenblatt, editor of The Jewish Week in New York, if I could write a different kind of column. "About two hundred words" I said, "if you think you could fit it in each week." After teasing me that a rabbi couldn't write only two hundred words, he agreed. For five years now, once a week, I have written the "Musings" column for The Jewish Week. It has been a joy and an education. The education has been in compression. Each week I cut down what I have written, try to trim what is superfluous, and stick to the point. Sometimes I succeed.

Judaism's lessons are both simple and complex. Most can be conveyed in an instant and absorbed over a lifetime. The lessons do not change, but we do.

The First Question

WHAT IS THE FIRST QUESTION in the Bible?

Before humanity was created, there were no questions. The first occurs in the garden of Eden. Adam and Eve have just eaten of the forbidden fruit. God calls out to them, *"Ayecha?"* "Where are you?"

How can that be? Does God not know where Adam and Eve are? For centuries, Jews have understood that this question has a deeper meaning. God is not seeking to locate Adam and Eve. That is why they do not answer, "We are over here!" Instead, it is a question of spiritual geography. Adam, understanding the import of God's question, answers that he was frightened, so he has been hiding.

That question is not only the first question; it is also the eternal question. At each moment in our lives, this question is addressed to us: Where are you? Where are you spiritually? Where are you morally? What have you done with your life, and what are you doing with it now? Are you proud of your conduct in the garden?

The first question is a single word, whose echoes are endless. *"Ayecha?"*

Where are you?

A REMARKABLE PEOPLE

❧

God found the Jews as one finds grapes in the desert.

~ Hosea 9:10

Embracing All Creation

∼

WHERE SHOULD WE LOOK to find Judaism's deepest values? Let's look at New Year celebrations. The calendar reflects the priorities of a tradition. The secular New Year is derived from the Christian tradition and is tied to Christmas and the birth of Jesus. The Muslim New Year is tied to the hajj and the founding of Islam. The ancient Greek New Year was tied to the first Olympic Games. The Jewish New Year is tied to the creation of the world.

Judaism could have dated the year from the time Abraham left Ur, the Jews stood at Sinai, or David founded Jerusalem. All of those would have paid fitting obeisance to the tradition. But just as the Bible does not begin with Abraham, Rosh Hashanah is not about us but about the world. Jewish universality is marked not only in the world but also in the world to come. "All the righteous of the world have a share in the world to come." That rabbinic teaching, repeated by Maimonides, is one more proof of our tradition's universal inclination.

So on the next New Year, raise a glass and give a toast to a tradition so embracing as to dedicate itself to celebrating the miracle of creation.

∼

Division Can Save Us

❧

IN *GUNS, GERMS, AND STEEL*, historian Jared Diamond asks why the Western world has come to dominate the globe. Why have aboriginal peoples been all but wiped out while the French have flourished? Since abilities are universal, what gave the Western world the edge?

Diamond begins by considering the distribution of resources, especially animals that could be domesticated. A place that had pigs and cows gave an advantage over someone living on land populated by giraffes and tigers. Part of the answer is geographic. A thousand years ago China had a decisive advantage in the world's resources. Though it did not attain dominance, Diamond explains that China was designed to be unified. Rivers do not bisect it; mountains ranges do not divide it as the Alps and the Pyrenees divide Europe. It does not have islands as significant as Great Britain and Ireland. Europe was destined to be divided, China to be unified.

When Columbus had the idea of a new route to the Far East, he took his proposal first to Italy's rulers. They said no. France also refused. He went to several potential sponsors in Spain before he succeeded. In China, one *no* would have scotched the whole enterprise. Division engenders innovation.

The divisions in the Jewish world and in the Western world are often a source of lament. But there is blessing in plurality.

A human king, teaches the *midrash*, stamps coins, making each one alike. But the King of Kings creates every human face, and no two are the same.

~

~ David J. Wolpe ~

The Daughters of Serah

~~~

WHO CARRIED THE JEWISH TRADITION from generation to generation? Whose unwritten wisdom sustains it? Our unthinking first response might be "the Rabbis." A more comprehensive, more thoughtful answer would be "the women."

The indefinable aspects of tradition—the feel of it, the smells of a home, the part that cannot be captured in words, that remain unwritten but indelible—were for generations the province of Jewish women. Their wisdom ultimately molded the character of Jewish life. We find this in stories and reminiscences. We also find it in the midrash, in the remarkable character of Serah bat Asher.

Raised in the house of Jacob, she lived through the slavery in Egypt. Her phenomenal lifespan is the tradition's tribute to the durability of women's insight. For it was she who first identified Moses to the people as the true redeemer—and they heeded her. It was she who told Moses where to find Joseph's coffin as the Jews left Egypt. Those mysteries were written in no book; they needed Serah, bearer of unwritten wisdom, to reveal them.

Finally, the midrash tells us, Serah did not die—she entered paradise alive. The legacy she represents continues wherever the tradition is guided, enriched, and uplifted by her daughters, the bearers of Judaism's enduring legacy.

~~

Receiving the Gift

There are plants in Hawaii that are endangered because their natural pollinator is rare or extinct. So men climb the mountains and go from plant to plant, pollinating them by hand.

In certain periods of our history, something similar occurred. The learned in society, the natural pollinators, became rare in certain climes. So scholars would travel from community to community, bringing learning and light. They would climb mountains literally and metaphorically to ensure that the nectar of Torah was spread.

Modernity has blessed us with both learned individuals and the means to transmit their learning. All the apparatus of modern communication, from printing to e-mail, makes the distribution of learning easy. The question for Jewry is not how to be effective pollinators but how to be willing recipients. The wisdom is accessible if Jews will take the time to learn. It does no good for the pollinators to climb the mountains if they find no plants there.

~ David J. Wolpe ~

Soul Clocks

❧

JEWISH EVENTS ARE NOTORIOUS for starting late. The clock seems to move all too swiftly for this people whose span is measured not in minutes but in millennia. So we are leisurely about beginnings. The Zionist leader Naḥum Goldmann once said, "I tried my whole life to come late to a Jewish meeting and never succeeded."

Strangely, however, Jewish law depends on precision in the measurement of time. Sabbaths and holidays have specific starting times. Ritual observances such as mourning have definite time-bound cycles. We seem caught between the rigor of ritual and the languor of social occasions.

Perhaps each clock counterbalances the other. Centuries of wandering do not always permit a fixed and insistent attitude toward time. Flexibility and patience are virtues cultivated by our uneasy history. Still, we did not allow tribulation to override obligation. For all the uncertainty in the world, there was certainty in our souls. Our spiritual clocks remain fine-tuned. Insistent on the rhythms of our devotion, we have also made allowances for the unpredictability of circumstance.

In other words, often it is a matter of finding parking.

~

Returning to Our Children

AFTER THE *AKEDAH*, the binding of Isaac, the Torah tells us, "Abraham returned to the youths" (Genesis 22:19). The Kotzker rebbe says this verse illustrates Abraham's newfound recognition of the importance of maintaining contact with young people. He realized that influencing them was critical to his mission. For he saw that Isaac, because of his youth, was willing to be sacrificed. The Kotzker says that Abraham knew there was tremendous power in the devotion of young people and that it had to be properly harnessed.

Every civilization has realized this truth. Young people are the ones who go to battle. For all the assertions about the egocentrism of youth, it is the young people, not their parents, who willingly sacrifice themselves in war.

The Kotzker is urging on religious leaders and teachers a great truth. In our young people are the dynamism and passion that Judaism desperately needs. Youth is indifferent only when indifferently taught, indifferently led. Moses reinforces this lesson when he proclaims before Pharaoh, "We will go with our young and with our old" (Exodus 10:9). Why the young first? As the rebbe of Ponovezh comments on this verse, "A child is an orphan when he has no parents. A nation is an orphan when it has no children."

It is time to return to our children so that they can return to our ancestors.

Connecting the Generations

~

WHY MUST THE BIBLE afflict us with genealogies? Even the devout reader's eyes may glaze over when the *begats* go on their endless parade. There is great significance, however, in those seemingly arbitrary chronicles.

Leon Kass, in his profound book on Genesis, *The Beginning of Wisdom*, reviews the generations between Adam and Noah. He notes that between the year Lamech (Noah's father) is born and the year Adam dies, all nine generations of human beings are alive at the same time. Remarkably, Noah is the first person born into the world after the death of Adam.

Noah is the first to be born into a world that knows natural death. He is the first with no direct link to Eden. As Kass beautifully notes, "Noah ... means both 'comfort' and 'lament,' a perfect name for new life seen in the light of inevitable death. These facts may explain, in part, why Noah would, uniquely, later find grace in the eyes of the Lord."

Genealogies are reminders of mortality, of the chain of generations, of the importance of each individual life even in the grand sweep of time. They connect one age to another and give us the assurance that we, too, will be remembered.

~

Measuring Time by People

HOW DO WE MEASURE TIME? In our culture, we do it by numbers: the Roaring Twenties, the 1960s, the '70s. Centuries are also numbered. We are living in the twenty-first. But in Jewish tradition, time is more often measured by people than by numbers. We speak of the generation of Abraham, the generation of the Flood, the age of Rambam or of Rashi. The Bible measures time not in years but by counting descendants; between Noah and Abraham there are ten generations.

This is part of the message of all those *begats*, which are seized upon as an unnecessary part of the Bible. They could be dispensed with if the Bible counted by numbers. But the Bible counts by people, not numbers. The value of time is the life that passes through it. Time is the measure of our deeds, our joys, and our sorrows.

The Bible deserves the title D. H. Lawrence once gave to the novel: the "bright book of life." As such, everything—even its measurement of time—is bound up in life, in the knotted, noble efforts of human beings to draw closer to one another and to God.

Who Will Live in Your House When You Die?

IN AN INTRODUCTION TO A POEM, Michael Blumenthal tells this story: "In Bali, some friends were asked by a Balinese couple: 'Do you have any children?' When they replied that they didn't, the woman then asked: 'But who will live in your houses when you die?'"

The Jewish tradition asks Jews to build families for precisely this reason: so that someone will live in the house of Israel when they are gone. As a people who have often wandered, the houses we've built have not always been on a plot of land. We have learned how to build a spiritual abode. We have built houses with words, with rituals, with Torah, with love.

Who will live in our houses when we are gone? Have we built houses for our descendants to live in? For we build houses not only for ourselves. "The great use of life," says William James, "is to spend it for something that will outlast it." The Jewish tradition outlasts any individual Jew. Or to put it in the familiar words of the Sh'ma: "And you shall teach these words to your children when you sittest in your house."

Looking Beyond Ourselves

✦

TWO CONSTANT QUESTIONS in Jewish history: What is our obligation to other Jews? What is our obligation to the world at large?

Rav Abraham Kook answers that the two are inseparable: "Love for Israel implies the love for humanity." Yet the choices of emphasis in one's life are often stark. At times of national peril we will focus on Jewish concerns. Great world issues will evoke a more universal response. The seesaw trope of Jews and the world plays through our history. Jews have always recognized, as the midrash teaches, that to drill a hole in one's own side of the boat dooms the entire vessel.

Among the fowl deemed nonkosher in the Bible is a bird called the ḥasidah (Leviticus 11:19). Remarking on the strange name, Rashi writes that the name ḥasidah comes from ḥesed, "kindness." Why kindness? Because this particular bird acts kindly toward its kin.

Some eight hundred years after Rashi, the Kotzker rebbe asks, "If the ḥasidah is kind toward its kin, why is it unkosher?" His answer: "To be kosher, you have to be kind not only to your own kin but to all."

∿

A Dialogue through Time

THERE WAS A TIME when little changed: People grew up in the same villages as their parents, knew the same people their whole lives, did the same work, ate the same food, and heard the same languages as their parents and grandparents. Today we are constantly meeting new people, hearing new philosophies and ideas, and meeting challenges posed by the shifting world around us. History has accelerated, and there is no turning back.

Judaism has been struck by the same acceleration. New ideas and new philosophies have flooded this ancient faith. In this bewildering array, is there a bottom line?

Rabbi Abraham Joshua Heschel once wrote an essay he called "Toward an Understanding of Halacha." It was subtitled "Jewish Law as a Response." *That* is the bottom line: If Jewish tradition is a response to God, then it can flourish. If it is an arbitrary mélange of customs, it will wither. But although Jews disagree about the history of our tradition, how it came to be and in what stages it developed, one idea must endure: Judaism is a dialogue, not a human monologue addressed to an indifferent universe.

We are all bound by the mitzvah of relationship: to God, to other human beings, indeed, to all that God has created. All those relationships are touched by the changes in the world. But in each generation, in each new context, the ancient and blessed conversation—the dialogue that is Judaism—continues.

Reaching Toward God

⌇⌇

THE TORAH PORTRAYS a reciprocal relationship between human beings and God. Contrary to our assumption, there is a clear suggestion that it is human beings who must first reach out. When the Israelites cross the sea and Moses cries out to God, God answers, "Why are you crying out to Me? Speak to Israel, and tell them to go forward" (Exodus 14:15). Then God will respond with the miracle of the splitting sea.

Later on Moses ascends Sinai to receive the commandments (Exodus 19:3). Only then does God call out to him. Or Hachaim comments that it is the nature of k'dushah, "holiness," not to move toward an individual until the individual has moved toward holiness.

Rabbi Abraham Halevy bar Hasdai writes, "Where is God? In the heart of all who seek." The initiative is ours; God's promise is response.

Some sound Jewish advice to one who wishes to experience God? Create a climate of sanctity. Make your table a tabernacle spread with prayer and discussion of Torah. Be mindful of holiness in your home. The Creator of all is the most diffident of partners: God waits, so to speak, to be welcomed.

⌇

~ *David J. Wolpe* ~

The Enemy Within

WHAT WAS IT THAT BROUGHT about the devastating attack of Amalek in the desert? In his book on Amalek in Jewish literature and consciousness, *Amalek: The Enemy Within*, Rabbi Elijah Schochet points out that the Ḥafetz Ḥaim believed that disunity in Israel provoked the attack. The name of the place where the people camped right before the attack, Massah (trial) and Meribah (strife), refers to the internal strife of Israel.

Rabbi Schochet goes on to recall the words of Rabbi Simcha Bunim, who observes that in the biblical passage "Remember what Amalek did to you in the desert" (Deuteronomy 25:17) the word *remember* is singular. Rabbi Bunim comments that it was because the Israelites lived singly, isolated from one another and uncaring, that they were vulnerable.

The lesson here is twofold: Both unity and the embrace of community are central to the stability of our lives and the continuance of our people. The very first comment about human nature made in the Bible is God's declaration that "it is not good for a person to be alone" (Genesis 2:18). It is not good to be alone as individuals, and it is perilous to be isolated as a community within the larger nation of Israel. In divisive times the title of Rabbi Schochet's book is particularly apposite; following a long line of exegetical tradition, Schochet identifies Amalek as "the enemy within."

The Double Struggle

❧

IN HIS AUTOBIOGRAPHY, *The Book and the Sword*, David Weiss Halivni makes a remarkable observation: Pondering the fears and courage that have marked his life, he notes that Jacob wrestled with the angel but was frightened of Esau.

Why did Esau frighten Jacob whereas he fearlessly faced an angel? Is it because Jacob was more afraid of God than of a man? Perhaps Jacob knew that God was ultimately merciful but Esau was unpredictable, violent, capricious—and wronged.

Perhaps Jacob's knowledge is the key to his fear. He did not wrong God, except inasmuch as he stole from his older brother. Esau was the living reproach to Jacob's sin. To be confronted with one's sins is frightening—more frightening, perhaps, than to struggle with God.

To complicate the question, the *midrash* claims that the angel was Esau's guardian angel. So in a sense Jacob struggled with Esau twice—first spiritually and then physically. For some people the spiritual struggle is more fearsome than the physical. In his book, that is Halivni's ultimate point, and it might be taken as an analogy for Jewish history: Though we could not always save ourselves physically, in our spiritual struggles we have been powerful and resolute.

∾

Without Roots, No Branches

⌘

WE ARE TOO PAROCHIAL. How often have Jews heard that complaint—and how often from Jews themselves? Why are we so focused on Jewish subjects and Jewish issues?

We should certainly look outside ourselves, and our involvement with the issues of the world is central to our tradition. But too many Jews contribute to every cause save those that touch their own people. Fearful of being seen as narrow, they turn their backs on home to embrace the world.

In his autobiography, Natan Sharansky tells of his Jewish compatriots in Russia who insisted that what was important was not saving Soviet Jewry but saving the world. Paradoxically, he writes, those who tried to save the world by taking up Communism ended up creating a slave state, while those who joined with the Jewish dissidents ended up playing an instrumental role in the overthrow of the Communist regime.

Sharansky quotes Cynthia Ozick's insight on the shofar. Ozick points out that a shofar has a broad end and a narrow end. If you blow into the broad end, you get nothing. If you blow into the narrow end, you get a sound everyone can hear.

∿

Who Has Hated?

DAVID MARKSON WRITES UNUSUAL NOVELS. Some of them are cunning compilations of information interspersed with his gnomic editorial comments. In *Reader's Block* the array is punctuated by the identification of various anti-Semites throughout history. In the middle of the page, he will drop in "Karl Barth was an anti-Semite" or "Kant was an anti-Semite." One passage reads, "Jonathan Edwards was an anti-Semite. While acknowledging that he had never met one."

The list is long and dispiriting: Roald Dahl, Degas, Kipling, G. K. Chesterton, Theodore Dreiser, Voltaire, Justinian, Chekhov, Saint Ambrose, Robert Lowell, André Gide, Chaucer, Toynbee, Juvenal—it goes on and on. Anti-Semitism spotting is the bigot watcher's equivalent of shooting fish in a barrel: It is too easy to be a challenging sport. The effect is to remind one that anti-Semitism is a disease for which education, talent, even genius provides no effective vaccination.

It also reminds us that the Sho'ah, the Holocaust, was loosed on ground that had been painstakingly prepared by generations of thinkers, writers, artists, and intellectuals, as well as by garden-variety haters. The world is not what it was, but it is built on what it was. And we recall all of those whose prestige or brilliance or elegance would seem to have made them immune to hatred but who brimmed with malice nonetheless.

We are too wise a people to be paranoid, but we are also too old to be naive.

Learning from Other Traditions

ONE OF THE GREATEST GIFTS to have come from the Jewish people is the Ten Commandments. Yet the Torah portion that contains the commandments is named after a non-Jew.

Yitro is Moses's father-in-law. He is wise, helping Moses set up a system of justice that enables him to ease some of his burdens. Once again, Moshe Rabbenu, Moses Our Teacher, teaches a great lesson: Torah can be enriched by truth, whatever its source.

Many great scholars of the Bible, past and present, have not been Jewish. Even some notable scholars of rabbinic literature, of the Talmud and midrash, have been non-Jews: R. Travers Herford, G. F. Moore, Hermann Strack, Peter Schaefer, and others.

The long and bleak history of the treatment of Jews in the world is painfully familiar. But we should nevertheless be aware of how much Jews have taken from the secular world. Without Aristotle, we would not have the philosophy of Maimonides. Without the Arab bards of medieval Spain, we would not have the poetry of Judah ha-Levy and Solomon Ibn Gabirol. In every age, Jews have not only contributed to the world but have also sought knowledge outside their own heritage. No people is so wise that it can figure out this baffling world alone. We are all created in God's image. Let us learn from one another.

Opening Our Hands
to One Another

TZEDAKAH IS A BEAUTIFUL MITZVAH — and a surprising one. Jewish law mandates that a beggar who receives Tzedakah must in turn give Tzedakah, for it is important for all of us to feel that we have something to give. But what of people who truly have nothing?

The Gerer rebbe asks a fascinating question: How did the Jews give tzedakah in the wilderness? After all, even though they may have carried with them material goods from Egypt, there was no need for such goods in the wilderness. And the manna fed anyone. So what was there to give?

His answer is to recall the midrash teaching that the manna tasted like whatever one imagined. Many Israelites in Egypt had experienced a limited repertoire of foods. So those who had eaten an unusual food could share their recollections. In that way, they gave tzedakah.

Tzedakah is often material, but not always. We give tzedakah when we share our imagination, our efforts, our love. In the Ashrei, recited each day, we speak metaphorically of God's open hand. We, too, must open our hands, our minds, and our hearts. Tzedakah is the gift God expects us to give one another. Giving money, while essential, is only the beginning.

The Differences
That Make Us Stronger

CONSIDER THE DILEMMA of Rabbi Moses ben Israel Isserles, known as the Rema. A scholar who flourished in the mid-sixteenth century, he was hard at work on a great code of law. In the midst of his labor, it came to his attention that the great rabbi Joseph Caro had already completed such a code. Caro's erudition and fame made the Rema despair that anyone would ever read his own: "I was afraid that I had worked in vain and labored for naught and robbed my eyes of sleep to no end...I was in a state of confusion for many days."

In time, however, the Rema saw that while he could not replace Caro's magisterial work, he could add to it. The Rema added sources, Ashkenazic practices (Caro was a Sephardic Jew living in Zefat), and dissenting opinions. As so often happens in Jewish tradition, argument bred intimacy; the two great scholars—Rabbi Moses Isserles and Rabbi Joseph Caro—are now regularly printed on the same page, with commentaries ringed around them.

The Rema could have published his own book, but he knew that differences, if they do not divide, can synthesize, giving rise to something greater. By allowing Jews to understand that differing thoughts and practices can coexist on the same page, these two great scholars set a model for the generations. Their book is called the Shulḥan Arukh, the Set Table, and it became the preeminent code of law in Jewish history.

A LAND OF PROMISE

❧

This land made us a people.

~ David Ben-Gurion

Coming Home

IN ROBERT FROST'S MARVELOUS DEFINITION, "Home is the place where, when you have to go there, / They have to take you in." Israel is a national home in just that sense. For centuries no place felt compelled to take Jews in. We were at the whim of others. Now we have a home.

The experience of wandering has woven its way into Jewish custom. It is an ancient practice to leave a corner of one's home unpainted as a reminder of its impermanence. The customary conclusion of the Passover seder, "Next year in Jerusalem," is another way of insisting that home is still elusive.

Yet home is not only a function of geography. In Jerusalem itself at the conclusion of the seder, we say, "Next year in a rebuilt Jerusalem." The home we hope for is a place without constant strife, without the pain and uncertainty that the real world brings. A real home is safe, and so far there is no perfect safety in this world.

Perhaps that is why home is so powerful in memory and in dreams. The home that was and the home that one day will be beckon to us. As the Ḥafetz Ḥaim says, "The trip is never too hard if you are going home." Remarkably, we have created a messy, fraught place that the Jews can at last call home.

Fighting the Good Family Fight

IS THERE SOME COMFORT TO BE TAKEN from the viciousness of Jewish infighting? In his book *Messianism, Zionism, and Jewish Religious Radicalism*, the Israeli philosopher Aviezer Ravitsky tells the story of Rabbi Isaac Ze'ev ha-Levi Soloveitchik.

Rabbi Soloveitchik lived in Jerusalem. Once when walking with a companion, he heard a member of Neturei Karta (who reject the legitimacy of the State of Israel) cursing the state. Rabbi Soloveitchik's response was curious: "This man is a Zionist," he said. "How so?" asked his friend. Rabbi Soloveitchik explained: "In Poland or Russia would he thus curse the authorities? Since he acts differently here, he must necessarily find a different essence in the Jewish state, a unique experience. Therefore, he is a Zionist."

Maybe only families that are essentially close feel so free to vilify themselves. With strangers we are more courtly, more diffident than with our own. In that paradoxical observation lies a seed of hope. We often get angriest at those to whom we are bound by history and destiny.

Of course, ultimately only families that can transcend vilification survive intact. The same heat that stokes anger might, if we choose, feed our love.

The Symbol of Peace

〰️

THE TORAH TEACHES US that when laying siege to a city, the Israelites were forbidden to cut down its trees (*Deuteronomy* 20:19). The deeper idea behind this law is the Torah's recognition that destruction is so much simpler and so much more final than creation. It takes an instant to kill a tree yet years for it to grow back again.

Have you ever wondered why an olive branch is a symbol of peace? Elias Bickerman tells us in his book, *The Jews in the Greek Age*:

> The cultivation of fruit trees, olive groves, and vines was also a valuable source of income for the agriculturist. But this was an endeavor for which peace was essential. When the enemy came, cattle could be driven to safety; if crops were destroyed, the land could be resown; but fruit trees and vines burned or cut down were lost for a long time. Indeed the olive tree, which flourishes in the stony soil of Judea, needs some fifteen years of care before it begins to bear its fruit, making the olive branch the most fitting emblem of peace.

The Torah's law reminds us that creation is sustained by the slow, painstaking, and devoted caring of human beings.

〰️

Have You Faced the Test?

⌒∾⌒

THE TORAH SPEAKS OF THE FALLING MANNA in the wilderness as a test. How so? Commentators advance various theories: One argues that the test was to see whether the Israelites would believe that they did not have to collect the manna on Shabbat. Another holds the test was one of gratitude—would forty years of being fed persuade the Jews to take manna for granted?

Yet it may be that the test was in the *absence* of manna. Once the Israelites entered the land the manna would stop falling. While the manna fell, it was clear that God was feeding the people. In the Land of Israel, growing their own food, would they still recognize that God was the ultimate source of all? Would the Israelites' pride in their own efforts obliterate their gratitude?

We, too, face this test. As we sit in the synagogue on the Yamim Nora'im, we are struck by the abundance in our lives. Will we recall its source? We did not create the bounty of the world, however much we may exploit and enhance it. Indeed, the manna never ended. Each day, blessings fall from heaven. The test is to realize it.

∾

~ David J. Wolpe ~

Holding History
in Our Hands

THERE ARE MOMENTS WHEN OUR HISTORY, our past, becomes real, becomes our present. Suddenly, like Moses on Mount Nebo, we stand and know that the stories we have been told are true: Before our eyes is the confirmation. We had heard, but now we see: Moses climbs his final mountain and looks out upon the land. The dream takes on borders, and the land spreads out before his eyes.

One reason we travel to Israel is to make that happen, to touch time. Lying deeper than current politics is the palpable reality of our past. Modernity is only the upper layer of the land; a land which is an expression of our immemorial soul.

My father tells of being in Beit Shean, in Israel, at an archaeological dig. He was leading a synagogue group, and a young man stood nearby not because he was interested but because that was the only way to walk through the area. A workman dug up a shard and was about to place it in a container. Instead, he handed it to the young man and said something in Hebrew. "What did he say to me?" the young man asked. My father answered, "He said, 'You are the first person to hold that shard in two thousand years.'"

Emulating Esther

OURS IS THE MOST FORTUNATE Jewish community that ever existed. We live amid the greatest wealth, safety, and security that our people has ever known. Why?

Our sages often discuss Yom Kippur in relation to Purim, so let us again recall the story of that festival. Esther fears approaching Ahasuerus. She lives in the palace and has a wonderful life, but Mordecai tells her that perhaps it was for just such a crisis that she was granted a royal position. Thus fortified, she speaks to the king and saves her people.

We are not only fortunate, we also have tremendous influence in the most powerful nation in the world. If we do not use that influence to help our sisters and brothers in Israel, to plead their case and present the truth, then we are as guilty as Esther would have been had she done nothing. Perhaps it was for just such a mission that we were granted this tremendous gift.

When Reuven, Gad, and half of the tribe of Manasseh inform Moses that they do not wish to cross the Jordan, Moses does not argue with them. He tells the tribes they may live where they will, but before they are comfortable elsewhere, they must fight alongside Israel (Numbers 32). We who live outside the Land of Israel may settle where we will, but we are not thus absolved of the responsibility to do what we can to sustain our people in our land.

~ *David J. Wolpe* ~

Remembering the Future

IN MASTER OF DREAMS, her moving memoir of Isaac Bashevis Singer, Dvorah Telushkin quotes the great writer as saying that what the Jews need is not only a memory of their past but also a memory of their future.

Here is a memory of the future: One day some years from now you are sitting at a bus stop in Israel. A young man limps to the bus stop and sits beside you. You begin to talk about life, who you are, who your parents were, where you came from, the synagogue you attended in America.

The man tells you that he was injured in the terrible years of suicide bombings, the time when people thought there would never be peace. He remembers those who helped in those years. Indeed, he remembers your home, your synagogue. Although nothing can take away the hurt, he personally benefited from the support that you gave. The people who helped him were funded by Jews in your city, Jews who cared. He wants to thank you.

What we do now will build that future memory. Let our Israeli sisters and brothers know that we have not forgotten them. Visit Israel, support it in any way you can. Act in a way that you will want a child to remember years from now. Let Israel's children know that they are not alone.

Takin' It to the Streets

SOME PEOPLE BUY A SUIT OR A DRESS and believe it is so precious they cannot wear it. Instead, they leave the garment unused, its value dissipating because its delicacy is overestimated. Sadly, we often do the same with the Torah.

The Sefardic scholar Rabbi Benzion Uziel believed that "Jews who had a deep understanding of Torah did not have to fear that it would be unable to withstand the pressures from non-Jewish culture…A living culture has no fear of borrowing and integrating concepts from other cultures; it can do so without losing its own identity."

This is a perilous time for Jews and for Israel. Gathering in study halls is not a sufficient answer. We cannot be a light to others if we ourselves huddle in the dark. It is time to take the Torah out of its refined wrapping, time to bring it to the marketplace, to the editorial pages, to the halls of power. We must mobilize not only the professional pundits but also our writers, scholars, sages, and rabbis, to remind the world of the durability and significance of our tradition. In the face of ignorance, indifference, or even hostility, raise your voice. Take Torah to the streets.

See the Difference

THE HUMAN MIND works in binary fashion: night/day, long/short, good/bad. Even subtle minds use this dichotomy for their evaluations: Charles Lamb divided humanity into borrowers and lenders; Max Beerbohm saw us as essentially hosts or guests, and Robert Benchley declared that "there may be said to be two classes of people in the world: those who constantly divide the people of the world into two classes and those who do not."

Judaism also works by *havdalah*, by separation: sacred/everyday, Shabbat/weekdays, divine/human. All separations are vulnerable to qualification: Light shades into darkness; the holiness of Shabbat colors the week. The Rabbis even attribute human characteristics to God. But the essential separation endures, and it is not a generous mind but a muddled one that cannot see distinctions simply because they are not perfect.

Israel is not a perfect place. Its people are not angels. Its soldiers are not all exemplars. Its decisions have at times been unwise. But to make a list of shortcomings is not to erase the essential moral distinction between Israel and her enemies.

Bringing Light
to the Darkness

⁓

ANNA WEISHBEIN IMMIGRATED TO ISRAEL from the Ukraine. She got a job as a waitress. Her first assignment was to work the Passover seder at the Park Hotel in Netanya. Now she is permanently paralyzed from the waist down.

Chen and Lior Keinan lived in Petach Tikva. They looked on as their two-year-old daughter, Sinai, played with her grandmother, Ruth Peled, in front of a supermarket. And they looked on as a bomber detonated himself, killing the child and her grandmother.

Those and so many others like them are stories, names, abstractions. But when we at Sinai Temple visited Israel recently, the names became real: the children in Hadassah University Hospital to whom we gave toys; Eldad, the Ethiopian Jew who greeted us from his hospital bed in halting Hebrew; Aviad, the soldier at Sheba Medical Center struggling to overcome the emotional trauma of his service. We held their hands, prayed with them, cried with them.

As we were leaving the pediatric ward of Hadassah University Hospital, one of our group said to a nurse, "You must be glad to see us go." "Oh no," she said, "you made that boy smile. He never smiles."

Sometimes a mitzvah is seeing for yourself and coaxing a smile from the darkness.

⁓

Have You Visited?

◦⟳◦

WHEN THE SPIES RETURN to the camp of the Israelites, they alarm the people by insisting that Israel is a land that "swallows its inhabitants" (Numbers 13:32). Fear spreads, and God condemns the generation to wandering. Remarkably, the Torah then recounts the rebellion of Koraḥ. What becomes of Koraḥ and his confederates? They are literally swallowed by the land—but it is the desert, not Israel.

Hidden in this reversal is a critical lesson of Jewish history. Right now there are those who fear going to Israel because it is a land that swallows its inhabitants—a place seemingly condemned to perpetual strife. But Jewish history teaches that in the absence of a state, Jews have been swallowed by the lands of their habitation. The twentieth century makes clear that it is not Israel but wandering that threatens to swallow the Jewish people.

There are difficulties in the Land of Israel. It has always been so. Read the Book of Joshua. When the people enter the land, it is far from the idyllic home we might expect. But apart from Joshua and Caleb, the spies were misguided. Israel is the best guarantor that the Jewish people will endure. We who stand outside the land must recognize the debt we owe to those who live there.

∼

GOD, FAITH, AND DOUBT

❧

*A Jew can be Jewish with God,
against God, but not without God.*

~ Elie Wiesel

Normal Mysticism

❧

THE SCHOLAR MAX KADUSHIN wrote a dense, rich work called *The Rabbinic Mind*. In it he coins a wonderful name for the religious outlook of our sages: He called them "normal mystics." A normal mystic does not have hallucinatory visions of celestial glories. A normal mystic does not spend days and nights in ascetic pursuits, conjuring up some other, arcane realm of existence. A normal mystic is not a cave dweller practicing secret rituals. He is normal.

Still the tag "mystic" remains. For a normal mystic is one who better sees, or feels, the shaping and guiding hand of Divinity in all things. No event, whether personal, political, or natural, is outside the realm of divine providential concern. The normal mystic is, in the phrase often used to describe the philosopher Spinoza, God intoxicated—drunk with the Divine. An awareness of God seeps into all the activities of human life until this unseen Presence is taken as the true foundation of being, more real than what we glibly dub reality.

To see God in the everyday is the legacy of the Rabbis. Normal mysticism does not escape this world; it elevates it.

〰

Seeing the Essential

✦

WHAT DOES IT MEAN TO HAVE VISION? The prophets and sages of our tradition had vision; they did not see or act like those around them. At times, no doubt, they seemed strange to their contemporaries. We can imagine the prophets eliciting the kind of remark that the poet William Blake once prompted when someone said to a friend of his, "I believe Blake is cracked." The friend answered, "Yes, but it is the sort of crack that lets in the light."

Religious vision means seeing beyond what is apparent. There is a blessing we recite each morning, thanking God for the marvelous workings of the human body. The *chatima*, the end of the blessing, declares that God is *mafli la'asot*, that in fashioning the human body, God acts wondrously, that God has fashioned miracles.

The author of that ancient Talmudic blessing was Rav Sheshet, who was blind. Imagine the vision granted to that sage. He did not see what was visible, but he saw what was essential. In his life and ours, Rav Sheshet let in the light.

✧

~ *David J. Wolpe* ~

Blessing God for the Bad

～

THE VOICE OF GOD IS IN STRENGTH, writes the psalmist, and that is often true. But we can find God in pain as well. Many people assume that in trying times, believers turn to God out of calculated or desperate self-interest. "There are no atheists in foxholes" is a smug saying, insisting that when people are in urgent need of help, they turn to God as a surety.

Actually, however, pain itself, the experience of loss, opens us to experiences of the world that we would otherwise miss. Hemingway writes in *A Moveable Feast* that when he was hungry, he understood the paintings of Cézanne far better; deprivation gave him a keener sense. Sometimes pain is the portal through which we can experience the reality of God.

The great Lithuanian poet Czesław Miłosz writes, "Man constructs poetry out of the remnants found in ruins." We are seekers moved not only by joy but by desolation. We find God in tragedy not as weak individuals searching for a crutch but as newly sensitized souls.

The Talmud insists that we bless God for the bad as well as the good. Some assume that is because even in tragedy there is blessing to be found. The blessing may be merely a catalyst, however, enabling us to use our newfound sensitivity to discover God's presence in the world and in our lives.

～

Causeless Love

∼

IN HIS BOOK, THE FOUR LOVES, the Christian theologian and writer C. S. Lewis argues that we are closest to God when we are least like God: when we are needy, downcast, emotional, yearning.

Contrast Lewis's view to that of Martin Buber: Buber insists that we are close to God not when we want something from God but when we want only God. We should desire relationship, not goods—whether they be wealth or favor or even health. True love seeks not gifts but presence.

Our prayers and sacred texts often give reasons for obedience: rewards, past favors, sanctions. But when the Sh'ma instructs us to love God, it gives no reason. The cryptic command recalls Montaigne in his essay on friendship, where he writes of his friend Étienne de La Boétie, "If you pressed me to tell why I loved him, I feel that this cannot be expressed, except by answering: Because it was he, because it was I."

We do not love the perfect person but love whom we love. We do not love God because of favors done but because of an emotion that arises from the fullness of our soul. As Rav Kook reminds us, the great sin of our past was *sinat hinam*, "baseless hatred." The great mitzvah of our time must be *ahavat hinam*, "causeless love."

∼

A Prayer for Beauty

❧

IN HIS FINAL YEARS the renowned rabbi Samson Raphael Hirsch one day announced to his students that he was going to Switzerland to climb in the Alps. "Why?" they asked in astonishment. "Because when I come face-to-face with God," mused Hirsch, "I know the Creator of the Universe will look down at me and say, 'So, Shimshon, did you see My Alps?'"

Appreciating beauty is an act of devotion. That is why in Judaism there are blessings for seeing beautiful mountains, the ocean, a rainbow, and other phenomena of nature. The Talmud advises that one should pray only in a room with windows. To sing to God and not see God's world is a contradiction.

In the marriage ceremony, the word *huppah* once referred to the traditional covering of the bride and groom, the *hupat shamayim*, "canopy of the heavens," what the poet A. E. Housman calls "the sky-pavilioned land."

In the Bible, humanity begins in a garden, and Judaism continues the use of metaphors from nature: It likens the Torah to a tree, the Talmud to a sea, the human spirit to wind. When we move through the world, we feel its rhythms, we are awestruck by its majesty, we absorb its beauty. We are doing more than paying homage to the forces of nature; we are offering a deep, authentic prayer to God.

∿

Can We Be Forced to Feel?

THE BIBLE COMMANDS: "You shall love the Lord your God."
But can feelings be legislated?

The question of nature versus nurture, heredity versus
environment, is old and perhaps unanswerable. But we are
increasingly aware of is the extent to which environment
affects genetics—nature via nurture, as one writer has it.
Certain genetic tendencies can be realized—or obstructed—
by our surroundings.

A recent experiment kept mice in darkness for the first two
years of their lives. When they emerged into the light, they could
not see. The gene for sight exists, but it has to be switched on
by the environment. Failing that, there is blindness.

"You shall love the lord your God." The Sefat Emet asks
how the Torah can command something that is "dependant
on human nature." Replying to his own question, he points
that that the answer is embedded in the question itself. It must
be in our nature, he concludes, to love God, but that love is
buried deep within us. The commandment is an exhortation
to live a life that will awaken that love.

The commandment instructs us to turn on the spiritual
gene that lies dormant inside us. Through study, mitzvot, and
acts of goodness, we can awaken the capacity to love one
another and God.

~ David J. Wolpe ~

Finding Our Own Place

THE RABBIS TEACH THAT THE TORAH is from God. Yet the most studied rabbinic text, *Pirkei Avot*, begins, "Moses received the Torah from Sinai." What is the difference?

The usual interpretation is that Sinai is a kind of spiritual synecdoche: It means "from God," and the mountain is a metaphor. But the great medieval commentator Abravanel proposes another answer: Had Moses not spent forty days and nights alone on Sinai, he would not have been *able* to receive the Torah. The time spent alone, in prayer and meditation, prepared him for the experience of encountering God.

The story is told of one Ḥasidic master whose child used to spend time alone in the forest. Concerned and curious, one day the rabbi pulled his boy aside and asked him what he was doing. "I go to the forest to find God," replied his son. "Oh, that's wonderful," said the father, "but don't you know that God is the same everywhere?" "Yes," answered the boy, "I know that God is, but I'm not."

There are certain places and times in our lives when we can find God. Moses had to have Sinai; the boy needed the forest. The challenge is to find our own place—and cherish it.

Floating Takes Faith

∽

IN A DISCUSSION OF SHABBAT, Adin Steinsaltz writes that we must do no work on the Sabbath—not even work on our souls. Yet we know that our souls are supposed to be elevated on Shabbat, that we should reach higher on Shabbat than we do during the week. How can that be if for the entire day we do not strive spiritually?

I remember when I was learning to swim. The hardest part was floating. Swimming is about propulsion: One must kick, stroke, move. But floating asks us to be still, to trust in the buoyancy of the water. Swimming is work; floating takes faith.

In the ocean it is sometimes necessary to swim, but the swimmer goes beneath the wave while the floater rides its crest. Similarly, the one who works on himself or herself all week should aim to float on Shabbat. Floating will carry you higher than the often strenuous effort of the week.

On Shabbat we are to consider the week's tasks complete: Shabbat asks us to trust the wave of God's world.

This Shabbat, do not work on the world or on yourself. Save that for the other six days, and when Shabbat comes, float.

∽

Any Eye for Mystery

WHERE DOES ONE FIND GOD? Jewish philosophers differ in their answer to that question. Some speak about finding God first in the eyes of another person. Some speak of finding God first in the mitzvot. Some speak of the wonders of nature: the sun staining the sky pink at sunset or the first buds of spring.

According to Rabbi Abraham Joshua Heschel, faith comes before the wonders of nature, even before relationships with other human beings. Faith begins in what Heschel calls "radical amazement," the sheer wonder that the world exists. Why is there anything rather than nothing? Who summoned this marvel into the world? "The world will not perish," writes the biologist J. B. S. Haldane, "for want of wonders, but for want of wonder."

Heschel enables us to understand that each moment invites amazement. Once we have the capacity for amazement, the world is a procession of marvelous mysteries ready to unfold. The novelist and poet Thomas Hardy might have been aspiring to the worldview of Heschel in his poem, *Afterwards*:

> If, when hearing that I have been stilled at last, they stand at the door,
> Watching the full-starred heavens that winter sees,
> Will this thought rise on those who will meet my face no more,
> "He was one who had an eye for such mysteries?"

Opposite Truths

◦～∾◦

WHICH IS TRUE: "Nothing ventured nothing gained" or "Fools rush in where angels fear to tread?" Which is true: "He who hesitates is lost" or "Look before you leap?" Pick one: "Out of sight out of mind" or "Absence makes the heart grow fonder."

Samuel Johnson observed that two things imputed to the human heart may not be logical at the same time, but both can be true. Each side of those paired proverbs is true at certain times. Human beings are creatures of contradiction; thus faith is often paradoxical. Judaism understands the wisdom enunciated more than a century ago by Oscar Wilde: A deep truth is anything the opposite of which is also a deep truth.

Therefore our year is laced with paradoxes: happiness in the midst of mourning, advice to cling to the past but never forfeit the future, certainty that we should expend all our efforts and energy on this world yet never despair that something lies beyond it.

Asked what constitutes a true Jew, Rebbe Menachem Mendel of Vorka replied, "Upright kneeling, silent screaming, motionless dance." Clasp all the sides of life whose raging inconsistencies will not allow a smooth, untwisted path. Nothing is absolute—not our kneeling, our screaming, or our dance. For as we dance, kneel, and scream, we also stand upright, motionless, silent, in wonderment at the ambiguities and fruitfulness of God's world.

∾

Holding On and Letting Go

❧

ONE OF THE MOST BEAUTIFUL SERMONS ever delivered was given by the late Rabbi Milton Steinberg. It was called "To Hold with Open Arms." In it, Steinberg describes emerging from the hospital after a long illness. Everything he sees touches him deeply: sunshine, the people striding along the street. He thinks how precious it all is and how careless we are about it most of our days.

Yet preciousness is only half the truth. The other half is that moments of preciousness slip away. We cannot feel unbounded gratitude all of the time. We must hold the world close, writes Steinberg, but know it cannot last. All poignant moments and beautiful things will pass.

How do we cling and still let go? The paradox is reconciled with God. Given God, Steinberg writes, everything is more precious, but none of it is ultimately ours. Only with God "can we hold life at once infinitely precious and yet as a thing lightly to be surrendered. Only because of God is it made possible for us to clasp the world, but with relaxed hands; to embrace it, but with open arms."

〜

Nomads and Farmers

WHY MUST WE BE BOUND by any one tradition? Can one mix together several faiths or traditions?

Rabbi Joseph Soloveitchik once made a distinction between nomads and farmers. Nomads, he writes, wander from place to place, grazing on the land. They do not love the land, for they cannot stay long enough to love it. They contribute nothing to the land. They take and move on.

Farmers, on the other hand, love the land. They work it, deepen it, live in relationship to it. While nomads wander at will, farmers wait patiently for the harvest.

Similarly, there are spiritual nomads. Some people are always moving, trying new faiths. They skim off traditions, but they do not love them, they do not contribute to them, they do not stay. To love a tradition and live it, one must be a farmer. One must plant, tend, nourish, and learn.

Judaism is deep and rich. Skimming its teachings will never lead one to know it and love it. Commitment takes time.

It is interesting and easy to be a nomad. You have a passing acquaintance with many things. None makes demands because no love develops. All it takes to be a nomad is curiosity. To be a farmer takes faith and commitment. Only a farmer can make things grow.

Awesomely, Wonderfully Made

❧

ONE OF THE DANGERS OF THE MODERN WORSHIP of science is the belief that everything is reducible to something else. Nothing is great, grand, mysterious; everything comprises collocations of invisible particles that together equal everything else, from barnacles to Beethoven.

The poet Joy Gresham (later the wife of C. S. Lewis) commented on her youthful views: "'Men...are only apes. Love, art, altruism, are only sex. The universe is only matter. Matter is only energy. I forget what I said energy was only.'"

The reductionist view of the universe not only flattens our wonder of what is but ultimately makes little sense. The world is far too complex, various, and enigmatic to admit of any simple property or explanation. Moreover, how can we be so sure that the mind, composed of the same simple matter, could understand both itself and the greater universe?

"God, I am awesomely, wonderfully made," the psalmist sings (Psalm 139:14). He is alternately afraid and uplifted by his own complexity. But he is never complacent.

A view of life touched by faith encourages us to avoid smugness and certainty. Those are the twin enemies of truth. Wonder, awe, and eagerness are its allies. As science advances and we see the wonderful unfolding of truths in response to the diligent application of the human mind, let that same mind have the humility to offer a prayer for the unfathomableness that shaped it.

∾

Seeking God
Through Pain and Joy

～

THE BIBLE GIVES NO ACCOUNT of how Abraham came to recognize God; that decisive step in Jewish history is shrouded in
silence. The Rabbis rush in with tales to fill the void.

One story compares Abraham to a traveler who sees a palace
in flames. He cried out, "Is there no one responsible for this
palace?" From an upper window the owner peeked through
to assure the frightened traveler that he is responsible. The
palace had an owner.

Similarly, Abraham, seeing the world in flames, cried out,
"Is no one responsible for this world?" God came to Abraham
in response to his cry.

The twist to this midrash is that the word it uses for "in
flames" is doleket. Doleket can also mean "full of light." So perhaps
Abraham saw the world as a blazing fire or as a brilliant light,
as a caldron of injustice or as a palette of beauty. Did he think
so terrible a world must have a monarch—or so magnificent a
world must have a creator?

Do we come to God from tragedy or from joy? The
midrash suggests that we come to God in response to both, as
did our ancestor Abraham.

～

The Beating Heart of Joy

IN THE STORY BEGINS, the Israeli novelist Amos Oz recounts that when he was in sixth or seventh grade a nurse entered his classroom and explained "the facts of life." She used diagrams and explicit language to inform and to warn the students of all the facets of sexuality. Oz writes:

> It turned out that the energetic nurse, who had no hesitation about revealing every last detail, from hormones to glands, nonetheless skipped over a marginal detail: She did not tell us, did not even hint, that these complex procedures entailed, at least occasionally, some pleasure. Perhaps she thought that in not doing so, she would make our innocent lives safer. Perhaps she had no idea.

Oz compares the nurse's lecture to critics who dismantle works of literature in ever more abstruse ways but do not know or communicate that reading stories is fun. Similarly, many religious Jews know the minutiae of Jewish tradition, but they forget what Martin Buber taught: "the beating heart of the universe is holy joy" that animates everything. They forget that law follows love. Perhaps they think it makes Judaism somehow less serious. Perhaps, heaven forbid, they have no idea.

Everyday Messiahs

～

IT HAS BEEN APTLY SAID that the history of messianism in Judaism is the history of failed messiahs. After all, if we are still waiting for the Messiah, then all the claimants to that noble title must have failed.

But there are messianic gestures and messianic aspirations even among those who cannot lay claim to the title. In his novel, The Days of Simon Stern, Arthur Cohen creates a character who seeks to become a modern messiah by saving the doomed Jews of Eastern Europe. Even in his lifetime, Theordor Herzl was hailed by some as a modern messiah.

The task of a messiah is to save, to redeem, to uplift the lowly, to humble the proud. None of those tasks, on a small scale, is beyond our capacities. We can undertake to be everyday messiahs, quotidian saviors.

"To believe in the heroic" says Disraeli, "makes heroes." Perhaps the most important part of messianism is the faith that it is real—not only ultimately in history but in our daily lives. The Messiah is not superhuman, just an exemplar of humanity. And this aspiration—to be such an exemplar—should not be alien to any of us.

～

Prayer as Poetry

WHAT IF OUR PRAYERS EXPRESS IDEAS that we do not believe?

Many people treat prayer like a treatise, picking through the siddur for doctrinal points. While we should not assert things we do not believe, we should understand prayer as poetry, not philosophy. The sound of the words, the rhythm and cadence, are integral to prayer. "Sometimes too hot the eye of heaven shines" is not the same as "Some days are sweltering." The content of both statements is loosely the same, but only one of them is poetry.

When we say *zot haTorah* as we hold the Torah aloft, we can recite the declaration even if we doubt that the Torah is the literal, verbatim word of God. For the declaration is deeper than definition. It is a current carried from the past into the future. "Beauty is truth, truth beauty—that is all / Ye know on earth, and all ye need to know," Keats famously declares. Clearly not if you have to balance a checkbook. But we do not read poetry for information; nor do we pray from the newspaper.

We pray to lift our hearts and stir our souls. Check your caveats at the door. In here we reach toward God.

Hang a Harp
Above Your Bed

❦

PSALM 119:62 READS, "I arise at midnight to praise you." The Rabbis asked a practical question about this verse and offered a beautiful answer.

Traditionally, King David is credited with writing Psalm 119. How, the Rabbis wondered, was he able to get up at midnight every night? Their answer: David, the renowned musician, would hang his harp above his bed, and at midnight God would send a breeze through the window to strum its strings. Roused from sleep by the music, David would rise to praise God.

In a modern Hebrew work, *Malchut Hayahadut*, Rabbi Avraham Chen quotes this explanation in order to teach an important point: What good is it, he asks, if the wind blows, but above your bed no harp hangs?

It is our task in life to ensure that we are alive to the possibility of the stirrings of God's wonder. We must train ourselves and our children to tune the instruments of our souls so that when the breeze blows we will be aroused by the melody. Hang a harp above your bed.

〜

Evolution and Faith

❧

THE CONTROVERSY OVER EVOLUTIONARY BIOLOGY remains at
fever pitch. Those who explain almost all human behavior by
means of Darwinian categories—scientists like Richard
Dawkins, Daniel Dennett, and Steven Pinker—are ranged
against those who see more randomness and contingency—
like Stephen Jay Gould and Richard Lewontin. Both sides
make eloquent cases for evolution, but the way evolution
works and its ultimate effect on human life are matters of
constant, sometimes vituperative dispute.

Can God play a role in this debate? Judaism does indeed
have a model for God's working evolutionarily. In the
Tanḥuma (Tanḥuma B, Devarim) we read, "When God's presence was revealed to the Israelites, God did not show forth all
His goodness at once because they could not have borne so
much good; for had God revealed His goodness to them at
one time they would have died....So God's self is shown little
by little."

In Nonzero, Robert Wright argues that evolution proceeds
by building up more and more cooperation and interconnec-
tion among human beings. In other words, human history
marches gradually toward a better end despite all the pitfalls
along the way; that better end is an inevitable outgrowth of
the system. Perhaps what Darwin ultimately teaches us is that
God speaks slowly through history. Perhaps some in our tradition knew that all along.

〰

Singing Masters of the Soul

JUDAISM IS A TRADITION OF WORDS, but it is also a tradition of song. In the Talmud we find an unusual legend: God ponders making King Hezekiah the Messiah but in the end decides that it cannot be.

Why? Because throughout Hezekiah's life God has performed various miracles for him. Yet through all the wonders and favors the king has failed to sing before God. Song must accompany redemption. One cannot be the Messiah if one's soul is fettered, if the heart is locked up—if one's spirit has no song.

In "Sailing to Byzantium," W. B. Yeats writes, "Nor is there singing school but studying/...O sages, standing in God's holy fire/...be the singing masters of my soul." The sages—in Judaism the Rabbis—are the singing masters of the soul. They mark the trail that enables a soul to soar. Sparked by holy joy, Judaism teaches a soul to sing. Without song, faith is a desiccated, hollowed-out shell.

As Rabbi Judah the Ḥasid wrote in Shir Hakavod centuries ago, "I sing hymns and weave songs because my soul longs for Thee." Through study, trial, ecstasy, and longing, Judaism continues to sing.

~ David J. Wolpe ~

Mountains and Microchips

IN PSALM 20:7, WE READ, "They call on chariots and call on horses, but we call on the name of the Lord our God."

Let us consider updating the psalm. Instead of reading it as a psalm about war, think of it as a psalm about daily life. Chariots represent technology; horses represent nature. In our lives we rely on one or the other.

Some revel in the wonders of technology; our data proliferate as our handheld computers shrink in size. Whether our faith lies in chariots or microchips—or any other products of the human hand—it is the same.

Others worship nature. Neglecting the less savory side of the terrestrial world, they deem everything "natural" as wonderful. That so much human beneficence consists in escaping nature—building houses, heating and cooling them, taking antibiotics—escapes attention.

There is wonder in technology, and there is magnificence in nature. We cannot live without either one. But to trust in either one alone is foolish. Thousands of years ago the psalmist left us this advice: Both nature and technology are imperfect. Rely on them only so far. We who appreciate both seek also to transcend both.

We call on the name of the Lord our God.

FORMING FAMILIES

❧

For this child I have prayed.

~ Samuel 1:27

Strangers and Brothers

～

AS THE JOSEPH STORY ENDS, we are reminded that one of its lessons is that brothers can become strangers. This is a story that is repeated every day, although with different particulars: Brothers go into business together and in a few years do not speak. Sisters who talk every day have a fight, and soon there is a strained silence at family functions. The Joseph story is one we know too well.

But the same story carries a hopeful message as well. For it is also about how strangers discover they are brothers. The brothers do not know that the viceroy of Egypt is in fact family; when they realize it, their world changes.

If we are lucky, we make a similar discovery. People who start out as strangers may not be members of our biological family, but through the years they become our family. We have discovered siblings in strangers. Those who are closest—spouses or best friends—did not always grow up together; instead, they began their relationship as strangers.

The Joseph story reminds us that biology is no guarantee of closeness and unfamiliarity no predictor of devotion. It is our task to keep families close and to expand them by including spirits who come to us as strangers and become our kin.

～

Learning Faith from Children

⌢

HOW IMPORTANT ARE CHILDREN to the religious life of adults? The maggid of Dubno answers that question with a parable:

> Once a father traveled for miles with his son to reach a castle. Whenever they encountered a river or mountain, the father lifted his son on his shoulders and carried him. Finally they came to the castle, but its gate was shut, and there were only narrow windows along the sides. The father said, "My son, up until now I have carried you. Now the only way we can reach our destination is if you will climb through the windows and open the gate for me from within."

So it is, said the maggid, with parents and children and God. Parents take care of their children, feed and clothe them, educate them, and see them through all manner of obstacles. Yet those same parents, who have so many strengths, often find the gate to God closed. But children have a spiritual magic. They can climb to places their parents cannot reach. They fling open the gates of heaven from within so that they and their parents can reach God together.

⌢

A Father, Not a King

❦

THROUGHOUT HISTORY, kings have had most to fear from their own families, particularly their children. Some wise kings have avoided it: Louis XIV said, "If I must fight, it shall be with my enemies rather than with my children."

Absalom, a son of King David, grew estranged from his father. Indeed, Absalom eventually rebelled and was killed in the attempt to usurp David's throne. But before that, David's agent Joab arranged a last attempt at reconciliation. "Absalom came to the king and flung himself face down to the ground before the king. And the king kissed Absalom" (2 Samuel 14:33).

Throughout the scene, King David is called king. Never David, never Absalom's father. Here is a subtle biblical lesson: At this last opportunity for healing, David acted not as a father but as a king. It was the king who kissed Absalom, not the loving father, not the David whom we know from other stories as a sensitive and caring soul. Later, when David grieves for the loss of his son, he might be recalling that moment when pride and position destroyed what remained of his relationship with his son. For kings as for all of us, when position intrudes on family, the result is estrangement.

∿

Never Too Late

⌾⌾⌾

AT WHAT AGE DO WE LOSE the potential to grow?

We tend to associate potential with children. But if we are sparks of God, those sparks are not extinguished with the passing of the years.

The Talmud tells us that Rabbi Akiba began to learn Judaism when he was forty years old. Despite that handicap, Akiba became the most renowned of all the Talmudic sages. In a similar vein, the Bible records the accomplishments of our patriarchs and matriarchs at very advanced ages.

We have parallels in other fields as well. Immanuel Kant, perhaps the greatest philosopher of the modern age, began writing the books on which his fame rests when he was in his fifties. Grandma Moses began painting in her seventies. What ties all such stories together is a resolution never to consider life—or one's own soul— exhausted.

When grandparents ask me how to influence their grand-children's Judaism, I tell them, "Change your own life." What could be more powerful than for a child to realize that a life-time of wisdom led Grandma or Grandpa to keep kosher, to keep Shabbat, to pray? And such a change teaches younger people a great truth: Learning should never cease, and neither should growth.

~

Memories That Endure

MANY INDIVIDUALS AND FAMILIES believe that ritual is too demanding given the pace and obligations of modern life. It is true: Structuring life with ritual is difficult—but very rewarding. A friend once told me that when he and his wife first married, they imagined Shabbat dinners at which their family would sit and talk and sing. The atmosphere would be warm and loving and the conversation filled with interest and laughter.

Then they had kids. The children made noise and wanted to leave the table and got bored—they were real kids, not fantasies. Indeed, it is rare for real live adolescents to name sitting down to the family dinner table as their favorite activity.

Now that my friend's children are grown, however, what do they say to him? "Gee, Dad, remember those great Shabbat dinners we used to have? Weren't they the best?" The discipline was hard, but it developed its own momentum and sowed memories that last forever.

In Jewish life for thousands of years, the force of ritual has created sacred moments that draw families together and, through love for one another, bring us closer to God.

Bringing Elijah

⌒〜⌒

I ONCE HEARD THE COMEDIENNE Cathy Ladman say that holidays are a time "to renew your resentments afresh." Surely no holiday gives us that opportunity more than Passover. Here is holiday friction in spades: the anxiety of preparing and cleaning; the gathering together for not one but two long evenings; the disputes over everything from why we left Egypt to the best seasoning for the soup to the right tune for "Ḥad Gadya."

In the midst of the tumult, we open the door for Elijah. Suddenly the meaning of Passover is manifest: It is about political and spiritual redemption. We were redeemed from Egypt so that our temporal slavery to Pharaoh could be turned into service to God.

What is redemption? What will happen when Elijah does come? The answer is found in the reading for Shabbat Hagadol, the Sabbath before Passover. The prophet Malachi teaches that on the day Elijah comes, "I will turn the hearts of parents to their children and the hearts of children to their parents" (Malachi 3:24).

So you see, if the family is gathered around and the atmosphere is filled with acceptance and love, Elijah can be there, too.

〜

Going Native

MY GREAT-GRANDPARENTS were strangers to America. They did not speak English well. They did not know the customs of their new land. Yet they were natives to Judaism.

My grandfather was not an observant man. But when they needed a tenth for a minyan, they called him because he knew how to daven, how to pray. He was a native to Judaism.

In our day we are natives to America. We understand the ways of this country, and we have had a colossal share in shaping its culture. But we are immigrants to Judaism. Walking into the shul, we do not speak the language; we are uncertain of the customs; we do not know when to stand, when to speak, what to say. We are as uncomfortable praying in shul as our grandparents were watching football in America.

Education turned a generation of immigrants to America into natives. Only education will turn immigrants to Judaism into natives. Even if lighting Shabbat candles seems strange to you, if you do it each Friday night it will seem natural to your children. Our grandparents learned English—the language of America—so that it would be the birthright of their children. Should we not be equally diligent in learning—and practicing —the language of Judaism so that it can be the birthright of our children?

Borne by Books

WHEN MY FATHER RETIRED after fifty years as a congregational rabbi, he dispursed his considerable library, and so for weeks my brothers and I received boxes of books. They are books I have always associated with my father; as a child I would run my hands over the covers and wonder what they were about and whether I would ever read them. Now many of them are mine.

There is something inexpressibly intimate about books. They are not only possessions; they are also a record of enthusiasms, aspirations, intellectual adventures. Many are gifts from people no longer in one's life; others, bought used, bear the marks of journeys taken before they reached the safe shores of one's own shelves. My father's books speak to me about the beginnings of my education. They remind me of my mother teaching me to read and my father buying me any book that struck my fancy.

My father's books sit in my office, and when I look at them next to my own it seems as if the generations are commingling. When I open one of his books and see his notes, I am reminded that our tradition is carried in words, borne by books, given in love.

~ David J. Wolpe ~

The Bible as Family Drama

~

WHY IS OUR TRADITION so preoccupied with families? We hear of the domestic travails and joys of many of the Bible's greatest characters, from Abraham and Sarah to Moses, David, and Ruth. If the Bible intends to legislate for humanity, why does it spend time with domestic squabbling? Why provide us these lessons in the intricacies of family life?

When the two most important analysts of the twentieth century, Freud and Jung, came to write their autobiographies, there was virtually no mention of their families. The tale each told was of work, not home. It is apparently easy—even for those with remarkable powers of psychological penetration— to assume that the only part of life that counts is the part we can manage, the part the world sees.

But the Bible is wiser. It recognizes that in the untidy reality of family life lies the seed of transformation. To change the world, one must seek to change living rooms and bedrooms, not just war rooms and boardrooms. To have a vision for the world means, in part, to have a vision for parents and children, for siblings, for spouses.

~

Why We Break a Glass

A JEWISH WEDDING ENDS with the breaking of a glass. The traditional explanation for this curious ceremony is that it recalls the destruction of the Temple; each celebration should be tempered by the historical memory of loss.

If we widen that idea, the breaking of a glass sparks a profound meditation on the nature of marriage and the inevitability of loss. The Rabbis teach that in a place of rejoicing there should always be a bit of trembling. For we know that each day will not be as joyous as the wedding, and only those couples who acknowledge the inevitable darkness will survive. It is not enough to be close in elation; when in the depths, those who love must hold each other more tightly still.

Not only individuals but relationships, too, mature through trial and difficulty. George Bernard Shaw beautifully says that, "The desert is a desert because the sun always shines." In order for couples to grow, they must accept the certainty of shadows, the lessons of loss. Under the ḥupah, at the moment of their greatest happiness, they make a commitment to something greater than happiness alone: They make a commitment to love and to the future, with all its perils, trials, and joys.

Good at Home or Good in the World?

❧

BEING IN THE PUBLIC EYE often entails a neglect of home life. The Torah reminds us repeatedly how difficult it is, even for the most spiritually gifted leaders, to keep the family intact. When we run through the litany of biblical characters who had serious family problems we are astonished at the names. Consider just a sample from the book of Genesis: Adam and Eve, Abraham and Sarah, Isaac and Rebecca, Jacob, Rachel, and Leah. Further on we find problems in the families of Moses, Aaron, David, Solomon, and many others.

The French writer Mirabeau, father of the famed revolutionary leader, was known as the Friend of Man. After his death his son bitterly remarked, "The friend of man was friend to neither wife nor children." The son's lament is typical. The spouses and children of the great and the famous often pay a terrible price.

In the Torah even the greatest of figures who neglected domestic peace suffered for it. That is why sh'lom bayit, "household harmony," is such a treasured value. Sh'lom bayit radiates outward. "One who creates peace at home builds peace in all Israel," says Rabbi Simeon Ben Gamaliel. Goodness inside one's home is no less exalted than greatness outside it.

∾

LEADERSHIP AND LEARNING

~

Learning is more important than action—
when the learning leads to action.

~ Talmud

Uplifting Words

◦~◦

IN THE FIFTEENTH-CENTURY BOOK, *KEVOD ELOHIM*, Joseph ibn Shem Tov tells of a self-regarding preacher who began a talk by saying that it would be divided into three parts: The first part both he and the congregation would understand. The second, only he would understand. The third, neither he nor they would understand. Joseph ibn Shem Tov adds that most of the sermons he hears fall into the third category.

Sermons are as old as faith, and criticisms of sermons are as old as sermons. "The good rain, like a bad preacher, does not know when to leave off," complains Emerson, voicing a sentiment shared by congregants through the centuries. Of course it is not only preachers who can be derelict. Congregants can hear words of great wisdom and ignore them. Marc Saperstein's *Jewish Preaching* records the sardonic comment of Leon of Modena—in the seventeenth century—that there was thunder and lightning on Sinai because God knew that when Jews hear words of Torah, they fall asleep!

Words can uplift, and they can sedate. But to have great poetry, as Whitman reminds us, there must be great readers. A sermon is a collaboration; it requires an adept speaker and an eager audience. Given both, words of Torah through the medium of the human voice can instruct and inspire.

~

How Do We Ignite a Mind?

LEARNING CARRIES ITS OWN SEDUCTION. Italo Calvino's story, "Numbers in the Dark," tells of soldiers sent to a library to purge unsuitable books. Soon they become so engrossed in reading that they are unable to censor anything.

There is a Talmudic parallel: The Rabbis tell of the convert Onkelos, who became famous for his learning; his translation of the Torah into Aramaic accompanies printed texts of the Torah to this day. Converting to Judaism was considered an insult to the Roman authorities, and soldiers were sent to carry Onkelos back to Rome. Upon hearing his reasons for becoming a Jew, however, delegation after delegation decided to stay and study the tradition.

One of the great frustrations of modern Jewish education is that it is often so thin, so flat, that it fails to ignite the quick minds of our children. Unlike the soldiers in the library, our children come upon an already censored, predigested Judaism, and it fails to inspire them.

The obstacles are many: Parents do not always support education, teachers are underpaid, facilities ill equipped, students tired from a day of secular studies. But we should let nothing stand in the way of igniting our minds and the minds of our children with an education of depth and texture. Judaism is not a smooth, effortless, always enlightened twenty-first-century religion. It is an ancient, knotty, deep, anguished, joyous encounter with God. It embraces religion, culture, community, land, and history. Only if we teach it as such will it be worth learning.

Repeating Great Truths

AT THE BEGINNING OF HIS CLASSIC WORK, The Path of the Upright, M. H. Luzzatto declares that he is not going to say anything new. Rather, he intends to restate truths long known, truths from the Torah. Although many are leery of hearing the same thing over and over, Luzzatto wished his book to be frequently reread. In traditional communities many people committed the entire book to memory.

Others have understood the centrality of restating old truths. André Gide once began a lecture by declaring, "Everything has been said before, but since nobody listens we have to keep going back and beginning all over again." Emerson, seeking originality, even grouses that "all my best thoughts were stolen by the ancients." The deepest wisdom always has precedent; it is not new but must be learned, relearned, reapplied.

We read the Torah over and over again because a truth heard once rarely changes us. Profundities must wear grooves into our souls. The Talmud teaches that one who reads the Torah one hundred times cannot be compared with one who reads it one hundred and one times. Perhaps the hundred and first time will make the text a part of our hearts and our lives.

We are constantly urged to seek the new. Most of the time, if it is worthy, the new is a restatement of old truths we neglected in our rush to grab hold of the latest expression of what our ancestors already knew.

Counting Cubits

TO THOSE OUTSIDE A LEGAL SYSTEM, the questions raised by the scholars who study it, may seem petty. A classic example is found in the Talmud:

> A bird found within fifty cubits of a nest belongs to the owner of the nest; if outside fifty cubits, it belongs to the finder...Rabbi Jeremiah raised the question, "What if one of its legs is inside the fifty cubits and the other outside?" For raising such a question, Jeremiah was asked to leave the academy.

Rabbi Jeremiah is known in the Talmud for trying to make his teacher, Rabbi Zera, laugh. Certainly the question about the bird, while it may have an earnest edge, also has an absurd one. But how exaggerated is it? Anyone who has seen the referee of a football game bring out a chain to determine whether one team has gained a first down realizes that the chain might seem foolish to one who doesn't know football; a great deal depends on it if you know the game.

Boundaries, property, speed limits, postage stamps—we live in a world in which generalities find their way into particular laws and practices. Our tradition represents the attempt to create a civil as well as a spiritual society. Our tradition recognizes that life can be a game of inches—or cubits.

How to Volunteer

❧~❧

PEOPLE WHO WORK FOR A SYNAGOGUE, either as professionals or as volunteers, know the joys and frustrations of seeking to advance the cause of God, Torah, and Israel in an institution. It should be easier: Are we not all devoted to the same end? What have board meetings to do with Sinai?

The French Catholic activist Charles Péguy says that everything begins in mysticism and ends in politics. Accomplishment entails the skills of organization, consensus building, and negotiation. It may be true that, as the old saying has it, a camel is a horse designed by committee; but the world needs camels, too.

Here is some advice from Rabbi Israel Salanter, founder of the Musar movement, which held that study of the Talmud must be accompanied by ethical study and ethical conduct. Rabbi Salanter said that while engaging in community work, one must make three resolutions: Never lose one's temper, never get tired, and never want to win.

Equanimity is a sign of respect. Energy is proof that the work is invigorating, because it is in service of God. Not wanting to win is subordinating one's ego to one's purpose. Rabbi Salanter reminds us that to work with others in service to something greater than oneself is not a necessary drudgery but a sacred task.

~

What Is a Tzaddik?

⌒∾⌒

THROUGHOUT JEWISH HISTORY some women and men have demonstrated greater sensitivity, goodness, or closeness to the source of life than others. The special quality distinguishing the tzaddik is ineffable: It cannot be distilled and captured. Elie Wiesel writes, "The tzaddik is no angel, no heavenly saint—the tzaddik is simply more human than his followers, and that is why he is their leader."

That definition follows the admonition of the Kotzker rebbe, who told his followers they must be humanly holy. "God" says the Kotzker, "has plenty of angels. What God needs is some holy human beings."

A tzaddik is one who makes the presence of God tangible in this world. The tzaddik limns the boundaries of human aspiration—it is possible to reach for a level of sanctity in everyday actions. Sometimes a tzaddik can make this tangible come alive even for the skeptically minded: The famed psychiatrist Karl Menninger wrote in his journals that while he did not believe in God, he believed in the tzaddik.

It was said of Rabbi Aryeh Levin upon his death, "For Rabbi Aryeh every human being was an entire world—and an only child." Perhaps no better definition of a tzaddik exists—or is needed.

∾

The Man Who
Couldn't Speak

THE BIBLE TELLS US THAT MOSES had a speech impediment. Why would God choose a man of impeded speech to deliver a message to Israel—why not choose a messenger better suited to the task?

Perhaps easy eloquence would have been too readily believed, requiring no act of faith. Conversely, perhaps God wished to show that the word was God's, for none would imagine Moses capable of such words on his own. Others argue that God wanted Moses to struggle so that God might teach him the trials of leadership.

Finally, perhaps the Torah is teaching us that eloquence is seductive but perilous. Listen to Sydney Smith complaining of the oratory of William Pitt the Younger:

> He was one of the most luminous eloquent blunderers with which any people was ever afflicted. For 15 years I have found my income dwindling away under his eloquence...At the close of every brilliant display an expedition or a kingdom fell, and by the time his style had gained the summit of perfection, Europe was degraded to the lowest abyss of misery. God send us a stammerer, a tongueless man.

In Moses, God sent one whose words were wrung from his heart. His speech was not easy, but it was earnest. Better than eloquent, Moses's words are lasting.

Body and Spirit

AS MANY *HAGGADOT* point out, Mitzrayim, the Hebrew name for Egypt, comes from the Hebrew root for "narrowness." In Hebrew as in other languages, many names and terms with powerful, emotional connotations are physical in origin. *Baruch*, "bless," comes from *berech*, which means "knee"— that which we bend in blessing. Ivri, "a Hebrew" in popular etymology, is "one who crosses over"; the name Yisrael is a product of Jacob's tussle with the angel.

As Emerson writes in his essay on language,

> Every word which is used to express a moral or intellectual fact, if traced to its root, is found to be borrowed from some material appearance. Right means straight; wrong means twisted. Spirit primarily means wind; transgression, the crossing of a line; supercilious, the raising of the eyebrow. We say the heart to express emotion, the head to denote thought.

We are corporeal beings. Our bodies are where we begin understanding and explaining the world. Even when we speak of the deepest spiritual issues, our language pays homage to our physical nature. We dwell in this world, and even when we contemplate eternity our thoughts arise from the dust of which we are shaped and even our spirit—*ruach*—comes from wind and from breath.

Breaking the Tablets

AS MOSES DESCENDS THE MOUNTAIN and sees the people dancing around the golden calf, he destroys the tablets of the law, given by God. How could he smash the tablets of God? Despite his anger at the people's apostasy, surely destroying a gift from the Creator should be unthinkable.

Rabbi Gordon Tucker points to a beautiful answer from Arnold Ehrlich's *Mikra Ki-feshuto*. Ehrlich writes that Moses was trying desperately to persuade the people to worship something abstract: They were being trained to revere a God they could not touch or see but whose majesty overarches the universe. Egypt had shown them only a pagan faith based on worship of the visible. Moses sought to educate them to believe in what they could not see.

Now Moses comes down the mountain and sees the people surrounding the calf. He looks up in horror at what he holds in his hands. Surely if they would worship a calf, they would worship tablets from the very hand of God. So Moses smashes them not to betray God but to fulfill God's wishes. Only if Moses represents God *without* an object will the people learn to worship God alone. They must learn that nothing in God's creation is divine, not golden idols and not even holy tablets.

Footprints on the Universe

SOMETIMES WE KNOW THINGS not by their presence but by their effect. In devising the periodic table, Mendeleyev reasoned that certain elements, though he had not found them, *had* to be there, given what he had already discovered. Similarly, for early astronomers the peculiar orbit of Uranus could be explained only by the existence of another planet, which was not spotted until much later. A more recent example is the pronghorn antelope, the fastest runner in North America. It runs much too fast for any possible predator to catch up with it, easily outrunning coyotes and mountain lions. Apparently, biologists have reasoned, fifteen thousand years ago the continent was populated by saber-toothed tigers and panthers that ran even faster than the pronghorn. We know of their speed only by the effect that remains.

The Talmud often preserves one side of an argument; the student must reconstruct the other side, hearing it through the patterns of silence. Unknown elements, unseen planets, and unheard voices leave traces. Nothing completely disappears; all that is and all that has ever been leave footprints on the universe.

A Home in Books

⁓

IN FEARFUL OR UNSETTLING TIMES, Jews study. To some it is inexplicable that worry will lead one to open a book. But for Jews, study has not been a simple intellectual discipline; it has been a form of worship, a refuge, a bridge to this world and beyond.

Why does the Torah begin with the letter *bet?* The question receives many explanations in Jewish tradition. Elie Wiesel answers it in this way:

> *Bet* is a house [because of its shape and because it begins the word *bayit*, "home"]. Thus we are told that the Book of Books is a shelter, a dwelling place. A place in which men and women laugh and weep, read and write, work and sleep. A place in which people love one another before they start quarreling—or the other way around. In other words, it is a home.

To study Torah is to enter a world in which we can be at home. Like home it is sometimes uncomfortable, too close, or suddenly alien to us. Like home, at times it forces us to live with people who irritate or upset us. But always it calls us back. Study Torah. Come home.

⁓

A True Disciple

WHAT DOES IT MEAN TO FOLLOW the path of one's teacher?

Rebellion is as common as discipleship. There will always be sharp disagreement over the proper way to understand the teachings of a sage. Who properly interprets the philosopher, the rabbi, the scientist?

Emerson, renowned for his concept of self-reliance, tore the leaves from his father's notebooks, from which the elder preacher gave pious sermons, and sewed in his own pages, which contained far less orthodox thoughts. Was that the act of a disciple or a rebel?

Perhaps an old Ḥasidic story can shed light on the matter. Two students were disciples of the same rabbi. Years later they ran into each other. One had developed his own interpretations with their own nuances; he had even developed some of his own practices. The other had slavishly followed every word their teacher had spoken. The meticulous follower was angry with his less punctilious colleague. "How could you do this?" he asked. "How could you violate the way of our teacher?"

The other responded, "Actually, I followed his way better than you. For he grew up and left his teacher. Now I have grown up and left mine."

Does Judaism Keep Secrets?

LEON WIESELTIER'S BOOK, *KADDISH*, is filled with learning and penetrating aperçus. On study he writes, "Analysis of tutelage loosens it. Understand authority and you have crippled it."

Power augments itself through hiding. Dictators are shrouded in secrecy, the Wizard of Oz cowers behind a curtain, and superheroes wear disguises. Religious authorities frequently rely on secret knowledge to maintain their influence. So-called mystery cults, relying on secret ceremonies, have always flourished, and faiths find it hard to resist the charisma of hiddenness.

In Judaism, although authority resides in learning, learning is not secret. To learn requires initiative, not initiation. Our tradition does not fear the spread of knowledge; rather, we are saddened by its scarcity. Even the recondite laws of the priesthood are revealed. The Bible meticulously recounts Temple rites, supplemented by extensive Talmudic discussion. Ours is a priesthood predicated not on secret knowledge but on precise public ritual.

Too much secrecy breeds clannishness and arrogance. Our tradition teaches us that while God is unknowable, the paths to God are open to all.

What Cannot Be Destroyed

❧

A RABBINIC LEGEND TEACHES THAT as the Temple was being destroyed and flames engulfed the entire structure, the High Priest took the key to the Holy of Holies. Desperately he flung the key up to the heavens. Out of the clouds came a giant hand that closed over the key and drew it back into the sky, to be returned when the Temple would be rebuilt.

Recently, in discussing that midrash with a colleague, I recalled first hearing about it from my father. My father had explained that what was significant was not the key that the High Priest threw up into the heavens but what he did not throw: He did not throw the Torah. No matter how great the catastrophe, the High Priest understood, the people would preserve the Torah. They may have lost the Temple, and they might lose the key, but they would not allow the Torah to be destroyed. Even in those desperate times the High Priest affirmed the faith that the Torah was given to us forever.

As Jews we struggle with the Torah in many ways, arguing over where it came from, what it means, how it should be enacted in our lives. But the midrash holds true in all respects: The Torah remains a Torat ḥayim; it is alive and gives life, and it remains on earth with the people who revere it.

〜

Knowing Where We Are

❧

BENJAMIN JOWETT, the renowned Oxford don and translator of Plato, was a paradigm of the ivory-tower scholar. Once when walking across the commons at Oxford, he stopped a student and asked, "Am I walking toward or away from the cafeteria?" "Away," said the student. "Ah," cried Jowett, "then I have eaten."

No less confounding is the story of Oliver Wendell Holmes, who was at a loss to produce his ticket when a train conductor came to collect it. Upon hearing that the conductor would trust the famous Supreme Court justice, Holmes responded, "My good man, you don't understand. I need my ticket to know where I am going!"

Our mental powers are remarkable. They permit us to concentrate and to obliterate. We remember books and forget people. We watch television and ignore children. We are unbalanced in our attention, sometimes to our advantage, sometimes to our detriment.

Perhaps we can leave the last word to another great thinker, William James. Upon being told that a certain man was absentminded, James demurred. "No" he said, "he is not absentminded. He is just present-minded somewhere else."

❧

When Legends Are True

~

MANY LEGENDS GROW UP around famous Jewish heroes. Inevitably the question arises, "Is that story true?"

An answer, in a story: Once the Ḥafetz Ḥaim was summoned to testify in a secular court. He was to be a character witness for a member of his congregation. The defendant's lawyer, wishing to impress the non-Jewish judge with the specialness of this witness, extolled the Ḥafetz Ḥaim and even told the following story:

"Once night, your honor, the Ḥafetz Ḥaim heard someone in his house. He hurried to the front room only to see a thief dash out the door with all his silver and valuables. Running out into the street, he called out after him, 'That property is *hefker* [ownerless].' In that way, you see, the thief had a right to the property and the act would not be a sin."

The judge smiled. "Counselor," he said, "honestly, now. Do you really believe that story?"

"I don't really know," said the lawyer. "But one thing I do know, your honor. They don't tell stories like that about you and me."

Perhaps not all legends about Jewish heroes are true. But the point is worth pondering: What sort of person must one be to inspire such a magnificent tale?

~

The Responsibilities of Power

IN THE ANCIENT WORLD, what was the traditional attitude toward power? When the son of the Persian king Cyrus, Cambyses, became king, he wanted to marry his sister. He called in the royal judges to inquire whether there was a law permitting the practice. They came back and said they could find no such law, but they did find a law saying that "the king of the Persians might do whatever he pleased."

What is the Jewish attitude toward rulers? A blessing tells the story. When one sees a potentate, one is supposed to recite, "Blessed are You, O Lord our God, Ruler of the Universe, who has given of His glory to flesh and blood." All power is derived from a higher source. Earthly rule is a human reflection of the majesty of God.

The Talmud teaches that during the Amidah, the central Jewish prayer, a regular worshipper bows at the beginning and end of two of the benedictions, a High Priest bows at the beginning of each of the eighteen blessings, and a king remains bowed for the entire prayer. The greater the temptation to pride, the greater the need for humility. The scepter is a call to recognize that human power is limited and all human beings flawed. True sovereignty is divine.

Visit the Past and
Discover the Present

L. P. HARTLEY BEGINS HIS ELEGIAC NOVEL, The Go-Between, with a now-famous line: "The past is a foreign country: they do things differently there." His words remind us that when we look into the civilizations of the past, we must remember that the contemporaries of Moses, or of Plato, or of Lincoln are not our contemporaries. We must judge them knowing that they knew things we have forgotten and that we take for granted things they could never have imagined.

Yet repeatedly we see the past as though it must be up-to-date. We smugly judge our predecessors: Their piety is fanaticism, their grandeur foolishness or barbarism, and their stories fairy tales. The loss is not theirs, of course. The glory that was Greece and the grandeur that was Rome—and the sanctity that was ancient Israel—rest secure against our refusal to understand.

Traveling, we say, broadens us as we come to realize that home is not the only reservoir of truth, or decency, or subtlety, or kindness. Well, as Alfred North Whitehead says, it is possible to be provincial in time as well as in place. Study history— visit the past—and discover a foreign country.

A Refining Fire

A STUDENT ONCE ASKED the great scholar Saul Lieberman whether there were any jokes in the Talmud. Rabbi Lieberman paused for a moment and responded, "Yes, indeed. The comment 'Scholars increase peace in the world'—surely that is a joke!"

Anyone who has studied in a university or an academy or a yeshivah knows that scholarly argument can be vociferous at best. Even in the back-and-forth of Talmudic disputation, ad hominem attacks are not unknown, and sharp retorts are practically the norm. Not even the greatest escape scrutiny— witness the famously barbed comments by Rabbi Abraham ben David of Posquieres on the writings of Maimonides: "Everything which he wrote here is vanity and striving after wind." "He has an overbearing spirit." "This formulation is darkness and not light." "This is great foolishness." "Here confusion reigns supreme." "This is clear falsification of the Torah." You get the idea. These are what Professor Isadore Twersky calls "gems of compressed disdain."

Yet the remarkable result is that readers of Maimonides knew his words had gone through the refining fire of other sages. They had been tested, confirmed. Ultimately the joke proves true, but with a twist. Peace on a small scale may not be increased, but on a large scale it is: The tradition is forged not through gentleness alone but also through sharp-edged intellects honing themselves on one another's words of Torah.

It Runs in the Family

THE ARTIST MAX BRAND was once asked why he was so enthusiastic about the *genizah* fragments, ancient, moldy documents that survived to nourish modern Jewish study. This mold, he replied, is the penicillin that will keep Jews from the disease of self-contempt.

It is learning that keeps us vital. The study of Judaism, the constant ever-flowing fountain of Torah, is the indispensable ingredient of continued Jewish life. No great culture can be built on ignorance.

There are more books on Jewish subjects published today in English than in any other language at any time in history. Is studying Judaism in Hebrew an important goal? Absolutely. But it is foolish to eschew study in English in the meantime. There are uplifting, important works of law, philosophy, scholarship, *midrash*, fiction, history, sociology, biography, and much more. They are waiting for us, mute if unopened, eloquent if read.

Judaism teaches us that God created the world through words. We are a people formed by a book. Read, study, learn.

At her bat mitzvah a colleague's daughter spoke truer words than she knew when she was asked why she so enjoyed reading Jewish books. "Well," she said, "it runs in the family."

Books Are Grand,
but Life Comes First

"PEOPLE SAY THAT LIFE IS THE THING" says the essayist Logan Pearsall Smith, "but I prefer reading."

Judaism is a tradition of study, but study alone is not Judaism. Books have their wisdom, but the world transcends what one can find in books. Martin Buber writes that he was content to spend all day in a room poring over books, but only because he knew that he was able to open the door and see a human face.

According to one midrash, when Moses and Aaron came to Pharaoh, proclaiming the sovereignty of God, Pharaoh consulted his wise men. They scoured all the books in the great library but could find no mention of this strange God. Therefore, they concluded, God did not exist.

That midrash is partly a message about knowing which books to consult. More deeply it tells us that consulting books alone is not adequate to penetrate to the core of things. Alongside study there must be encounter; next to learning must be living.

Spinning books into more books, words into more words, is a temptation for those who love Judaism's intellectually charged tradition. But the midrash presages the wise words of Thoreau two thousand years later: "How vain it is to sit down to write" he admonishes in *Walden*, "when you have not stood up to live." Books are grand, but life comes first.

Saving the Message

⟨ornament⟩

ISAAC ASIMOV'S CLASSIC *FOUNDATION* trilogy tells of a man named Hari Seldon, who, envisioning the coming apocalypse, creates a haven in which to build a great encyclopedia of human knowledge. This seemingly simple task hides a much grander scheme, and the underlying message is Seldon's abiding faith that knowledge coupled with wisdom can save us from the abyss.

There was also a Seldon in Jewish history. As the Talmud tells the story, while Jerusalem burned, Rabbi Johanan ben Zakkai was smuggled out in a coffin. At the Roman camp he entreated the future emperor Vespasian to give him "Yavneh and its sages." In other words, he wanted to build a colony, like Seldon's planet, Terminus, in which to preserve the knowledge of the ages.

Like Asimov's fictional hero, Yohanan ben Zakkai had a greater aim in mind—greater than Vespasian could imagine. He prepared for a time when there would be no more empire, but the Jewish people, its tradition intact, would bring the essential message of God to the surviving world.

⟨ornament⟩

How Do You *Tend Sheep?*

⸙

WHEN SAMUEL IS DISPATCHED to the house of Jesse to find a new king, he meets David, who has been tending sheep. Moses, too, was a shepherd, as was Jacob before him. The Rabbis wryly note this, saying that "when God wishes to find a leader, God looks to see how he tends sheep."

If you want to find someone to lead, don't look to see how he or she treats the rich or the powerful. To be rich or powerful means to be able to command the loyalty, or at least the aid, of others. A leader has to care for those who are powerless, those who are alone, those who are bereft. The prophets continually insisted that Israel would be judged by its treatment of the widow and the orphan. Upon hearing that he would not be able to enter the land of Israel, what was Moses's first reaction? He pleaded with God to find someone else to lead the people so that the nation would not be "like sheep that have no shepherd."

That plea was a vindication of what we might call the shepherd principle of selection. Moses cared deeply for the people, praying to God to ensure that his flock would arrive safely in the Promised Land.

⸰

Logic Is Neat,
But Life Is Messy

SHERLOCK HOLMES AND STAR TREK'S Spock remind us of the
blinding power of pure logic. The stories are contrived but
convincing—if only we could reason like that! Yet there are
some marvelous mysteries that depend on the masterly detective
getting things wrong. In Ronald Knox's *Viaduct Murder* and
most famously in E. C. Bentley's *Trent's Last Case*, the detective
follows a careful train of argument, meticulously reasoned,
that proves entirely mistaken. Logic is a shaky tool in human
affairs. As Kohelet puts it, "God made men forthright, but they
have engaged in too much reasoning" (Ecclesiastes 7:29).

That is a striking adage for a tradition so devoted to logic
and analysis. But analytic acuity, though impressive enough to
give the impression of infallibility, is only one tool for arriving
at the truth. Does anyone really suppose that professors of
logic are on the whole more effective or exact in their estimates
of human nature and conduct than stonemasons or poets?

Logic is neat, but life is messy. Judaism certainly esteems
argument, deduction, logical analysis: We even include the
rules of Talmudic reasoning in our morning prayers. Still, life
overspills boundaries, and logic must yield to wisdom. Thank
God.

Socrates versus the Talmud

MUCH OF TALMUDIC DISCOURSE is built on the mahloket, the "disagreement" or "argument." One of my Talmud teachers told me that as a child in yeshivah, when he was not paying attention during Talmud class and the teacher would ask about a certain passage, he would always answer, "There's a mahloket," and invariably he would be right.

In a Talmudic study hall, students sit across from each other in pairs, asking and answering each other in a crescendo of intellectual virtuosity. This is a fair fight between equals, not the Socratic dialogue of much American education. As Max Beerbohm caustically remarks, the Socratic dialogue is not a game at which two can play: A teacher asks the questions and leads the student, gently or otherwise, to the correct answer. In the Talmudic dispute, however, either party can pull in other sources, quote the speaker against himself (raminhu, literally "throw him against himself," that is, seek a contradiction), and the answer, though important, takes a backseat to the process.

The lesson is that among God's gifts are the majesty of our minds and the complexity of God's word and God's world. Talmud Torah k'neged kulam, "study of Torah is equal to all of the other mitzvot." Because it is in the processes of dispute, clarification, learning, and finally understanding—the vigorous play of the mind—that we seek to fathom the mysteries that God has bestowed upon us.

SPIRITUAL GROWTH

❧ ⌘ ❧

The sole aim of the mitzvot is to refine human nature.

~ Talmud

❧ ⌘ ❧

The Beauty of Humility

THERE IS A POWERFUL CHARACTER trait that is not merely undervalued in this country but positively derided. Our tradition calls it *anavah*. The English word is "humility."

The only character description of Moses in the Torah is that he is the most humble man on earth. The Rabbis declare that the Torah was given on Sinai, a small mountain, to teach humility. A later scholar asks why, if the lesson is humility, was the Torah not given in a valley? The answer is that the idea is not to teach humility in one without merit; instead, to be a mountain, to have gifts, to burst with talent, and still to be humble—that is an achievement.

A characteristic that strikes anyone who watches contemporary "reality television" is that each participant is encouraged to boast of his or her qualities. Humility is equivalent to low self-esteem, the great failing in prime-time land. "Who is wise? One who learns from all people." That rabbinic teaching does not resonate in a society in which music is boasting to a beat and politics is the art of announcing why the magnitude of a candidate's gifts has persuaded him or her to take office and save the civilized world.

A tzaddik once said, "If the Messiah should come and say to me, 'You are better than others,' I would say, 'You are not the Messiah.'"

Humility is a beautiful virtue. True humility is not a reflection of the certainty that we are worthless; it is a reflection of the certainty that we are invaluable, blessed, fashioned in the image of God.

Between Hearts and Heaven

IN JACOB'S DREAM, why do the angels who ascend and descend need a ladder? Aren't angels able to fly?

The angels and their ladder teach us that realizing dreams requires a step-by-step approach. Ascent is not quick. While they take just a moment to conceive, dreams demand time and effort to achieve. The ladder is rich in symbolism: Not only does it remind us that reaching toward heaven is often a rung-by-rung process, but it may be climbed in either direction.

Asked what God has been doing since the completion of creation, Rabbi José ben Halafta replied that God has been building ladders for some to ascend and others to descend.

Yeats wrote, "Now that my ladder's gone,/I must lie down where all the ladders start,/In the foul rag-and-bone shop of the heart." Jacob lay down and found a ladder. It began in the foul rag–and-bone shop of the heart, but it stretched to the heavens. Between heaven and the human heart, God has offered us a ladder.

Why Do We Bow?

ONE CAN LEARN THE TRUTH about spiritual growth from a ram's horn.

The shofar call begins with a *tekiah*, a long, unbroken blast; progresses to *sh'varim*, three wailing blasts; and finally reaches the staccato *t'ru'ah*. But the shofar always returns to the *t'ki'ah*. That is the growth of a spirit: first wholeness; then brokenness, shattering; and finally a new, stronger wholeness.

Bowing teaches the same lesson: We begin standing upright, bow down, and again stand upright. At the end of the Amidah prayer, we even raise our heels as if to say, "I am higher now than when I began, for in the meantime I have bowed low."

"Life breaks all of us," writes Hemingway. "Some grow strong at the broken places." That is wisdom the Rabbis knew and have taught for generations. We grow not only through triumph but also through failure, humility, and even doubt. As the Talmud teaches, "One cannot acquire Torah who has not failed in it."

Judaism embodies the wisdom of paradox: By bowing, we are uplifted; by being broken, we can emerge whole.

Get Some Sleep

DOCTORS TELL US THAT MOST AMERICANS do not get enough sleep. Why not? In part because we are too busy, but in part because we are ambivalent about sleep. We need sleep, even enjoy it, yet we think it a weakness or a waste of time.

Jewish tradition is also ambivalent toward sleep. It is often a divine blessing. The psalmist writes, "He grants his beloved sleep" (Psalms 127:2). Untroubled sleep is generally seen as a sign of an untroubled mind. Yet sleep has, if you will, a dark side.

Sleep is first mentioned in the Bible when God puts Adam to sleep. One *midrash* claims that act is the beginning of humanity's downfall (*Genesis Rabbah* 17:5). The Talmud proclaims that sleep is one-sixtieth of death (*Berakhot* 57b). Bedtime prayers remind us of the fear sleep often arouses in us; in times of crisis, the Rabbis fancifully imagine, even God's sleep is disturbed (*Pirkei de Rabbi Eliezer* 50).

The final verdict? Ultimately perhaps our attitude toward sleep is decisive. The adage never to go to bed fighting has its parallel in our prayers. The Hashkiveinu, the evening prayer for peace, reads, "Cause us to lie down in peace and rise up again to life." Why does the prayer begin with lying down? Because how we lie down can determine how we rise up. So sleep well, and rise in peace.

Fear of Falling

∿

LIFE CAN SLIP OUT FROM BENEATH us without our noticing. At times we work so hard and focus so intently that we do not realize what we are missing. Some people I know remind me of Wile E. Coyote in the *Road Runner* cartoons, who is forever running off the cliff. So long as his feet keep moving, he remains suspended in midair. But the moment he looks down—the moment he realizes there is no foundation under his feet—he falls.

Perhaps we run so quickly because we are afraid of falling. Is there a foundation under our feet? Have we built our foundation with the bricks of human love, learning, and wisdom? Or is the race so swift because the goal grows ever less certain?

Jewish life is a brake on our activities: It seeks to slow us down. On Shabbat we are not running. If we make a blessing before and after meals, we cannot exactly eat on the fly. For a little while, Judaism counsels, stop running. See what is beneath your feet. Find your support in this world. Then you can move forward again, this time with the certainty that you are getting somewhere.

∿

Writing Our Own Torah

JEWISH LAW ENJOINS EACH INDIVIDUAL to write a Sefer Torah. This injunction applies "even if your parents have bequeathed one to you." We are not to write the Sefer Torah in order to possess one physically. We are enjoined not to own a Torah scroll but rather to write one.

Our lives are parchment, our deeds the words. At each moment we determine the style and content of the scroll. Our masterworks are written in deeds; even those who write for a living must find their inspiration and guidance in life.

If we aim high, we can aspire to write a Torah with our lives. When Rabbi Eliezer the Great died, the Talmud tells us, as he was buried, the mourners said, "A Torah scroll is being hidden away." His life was so perfect an embodiment of the ideals of our tradition that it was as if he had become a Torah. To some are given the talent and training to write a Torah scroll on parchment. To all of us is it given to write a sacred story against the backdrop of our lives.

Pooh's Moons

WHEN MY DAUGHTER WAS TWO YEARS OLD, she gave me a glimpse into the origins of art. She was identifying parts of her Winnie-the-Pooh doll for me, pointing and saying, "This is Winnie-the-Pooh's nose; these are Winnie-the-Pooh's eyes," and so on. When she reached his eyebrows, she said without pausing, "These are Winnie-the-Pooh's moons." For her the crescent shape was a moon, and it never occurred to her to think otherwise.

I remember reading Richard Feynman's argument that innovation in science is the province of the young because the young haven't learned too much yet. Ideas are often the product of immersion in learning, but they can also be the wild children of fresh perspectives. To turn those ideas into art or science takes discipline, learning, and time. Still, we should celebrate the initial impulses that mark inventiveness.

Freud once wrote that the world cannot do without those who are willing to think new thoughts before they can prove them. New images, new thoughts, and even new truths can sometimes be the gift of those who have not yet mastered the old ones.

Visiting the Sick

❧

THE BIBLE RELATES that after Abraham's circumcision, God came to visit him. That is the first example of bikur ḥolim, the great mitzvah of visiting those who are ill.

The curious wording of the passage leads to a clever interpretation by the Amshinover rebbe. The Bible tells us that "The Lord appeared" to Abraham (Genesis 18:1). Yet in the next verse it says, "Looking up, Abraham saw three men." The tradition understands the three men to be angels, one of whom was specially sent to cure Abraham. But, notes the Amshinover rebbe, God had already visited, so why did an angel have to cure Abraham? Why had God not cured him first?

The rebbe's answer is that God was performing the mitzvah of bikur ḥolim. God was visiting Abraham as a friend. God did not wish to turn the visit into a professional one by acting as the divine doctor.

In that tongue-in-cheek exegesis we learn an important lesson: Bikur ḥolim is about the warmth of our presence; it is about bringing ourselves to someone who is ill. It does not require that we bring a cure. It requires only that we hold the hand of one who is ill and, through our presence, show our love.

〰

From Dreams to Mission

⌒∼⌒

HAVE WE GROWN INTO THE PEOPLE we were meant to be? Have we realized our capacities in this world, or have we betrayed our potential? Those are difficult questions, to be answered in the privacy of our own soul.

At times we are lucky enough to receive hints from outside ourselves as well. The story is told of Rabbi Chaim of Volozhin, a renowned scholar, that he was an indifferent student. One day he decided to abandon his studies and go to a trade school. He announced his decision to his parents, who reluctantly acquiesced.

That night the young man had a dream. In it he saw an angel holding a stack of beautiful books. "Whose books are those?" he asked the angel. "They are yours," was the answer, "if you have the courage to write them." The dream changed the young man's life, and Rabbi Chaim of Volozhin was on his way to discovering who he was meant to become.

One aspect of taking ourselves seriously is interrogating the state of our souls, asking where we are and where we might be. At times our dreams give us a hint that what we have done in our lives is but a prelude.

∼

The Word
That Gives Freedom

~

THERE IS A SINGLE WORD that grants freedom to human beings. That word is no.

We often think of Judaism as a religion that is filled with affirmation: We say yes to life, to love, to the pleasures of the world. Indeed, in the Jerusalem Talmud (Kid, 2:65) we are admonished that we will be "held to account for all the pleasures that our eyes beheld in this world but in which we did not partake." That seemingly libertine statement is often quoted to prove that Judaism is a tradition just this side of genuine hedonistic license, one full of healthy affirmations.

But Judaism is also full of negation. Our tradition repeatedly instructs us in the liberating art of saying no. Souls that cannot say no are undisciplined and thus ultimately unable to utter a true yes. Parents who do not set boundaries for their children do not raise free children but instead raise chaotic, unstable ones. Boundaries are the frame that define the painting.

In Jewish history there have been pious men and women who deprived themselves, who fasted and renounced many of the pleasures of the world. To dismiss them as fanatic or unhealthy misses the crucial point: To take one's soul seriously is to be able to say no.

~

Courage

~∾~

WE KNOW THAT TO MAKE PEACE requires courage—and not just the passive avoidance of conflict. Again and again in this world we see tyrants triumph when others refuse to speak up.

For a long time the crimes of Stalin were not mentioned in the Soviet Union. The taboo was first officially broken by Nikita Kruschev in a secret seven-hour speech in the Politburo, chronicling the dictator's crimes. In the midst of his speech, a voice was heard from the back of the chamber: "Comrade, where were you when all of this was going on?" Kruschev demanded that the questioner identify himself. No one stood up. "Comrade," said Kruschev, "that's where I was."

Heroes in Jewish history who have demanded justice have also loved peace. Remaining silent in response to intimidation is not an affirmation of peace but a reflex of fear. When Abraham cries out before God, "Shall the Judge of all the earth not do justice?" (Genesis 18:25), it is so that when later generations ask, "Where were you?" he will not have to say, "I was frightened, so I was silent."

~∾~

Igniting a Spark

RABBI ABRAHAM JOSHUA HESCHEL used to tell the story of the blacksmith who apprenticed to the master. He worked hard to perfect his craft. In time he took over the trade, but his customers dwindled away. He went to the rabbi and asked why.

The rabbi told him, "My child, you have learned your trade well. You can forge the metal, place the anvil, strike a smart blow with the hammer. But, alas, you have not learned to kindle the spark."

Technique is no substitute for passion. In our lives there must be an animating spark, something that moves us beyond the mundane, something that encourages us to transcend ourselves. Parenting books don't make a parent any more than cookbooks make a cook. To create something that is alive, something that is warm, you need a spark.

I wonder what happened to that poor blacksmith. I hope that he went somewhere quiet and meditated on what he really cared about in this world. I hope he found something that moved and changed him. I hope that when the rabbi next met him, he was shocked to see a new blacksmith, a man lit up from within, a soul on fire.

Does Suffering Breed Compassion?

SUFFERING IS SAID TO MAKE A PERSON compassionate. Yet are the downtrodden truly kinder than the favored? Experience proves that affliction, reputedly the school of compassion, often hardens the character. Suffering can make people coarse and unkind, can enable them to feel victimized even when they are victimizing others.

In James Gould Cozzens's dyspeptic novel, By Love Possessed, a disabled character, Julius Penrose, says, "Never believe that afflictions improve character, enlarge the understanding, or teach you charitable thoughts! The man not afflicted, the easy, open, fortunate man is the likable man, the kindly man, the considerate man—in short, the man who may have time and inclination to think of someone besides himself."

The Torah's constant admonition to the Israelites to be kind for they have suffered is perhaps not advice to act in character but rather to act out of character. Even though you have suffered, even though you might as a result be hard and cruel—be kind! Your own pain, teaches the Torah, is no excuse, however much you may be inclined to excuse yourself because of it. Suffering is not an assurance of decency but a challenge to it; in rising above the challenge, we prove ourselves most profoundly holy.

Does God Root for Our Team?

RECENTLY THE *LOS ANGELES TIMES* ran a feature on its sports page: "Does God Care Who Wins?" It quoted a number of athletes making appalling pronouncements about God favoring their team. It recalled the long tradition of prayers for victory that distinguish not only professional teams but also colleges teams, such as Notre Dame's.

To proclaim God's partisanship for sports teams is not only a trivialization of the Divine but also a monstrous display of hubris. Why should God love one team more than another? Is it the stadium that catches God's eye? The uniforms? Maybe God just likes a strong defense.

Yet we often make similar claims when it comes to our own convictions or our own people. Does God favor the Jews because they are Jews? Is our "team" automatically to be preferred? The prophet Amos said in God's name, "True, I brought Israel up from the land of Egypt, but also the Philistines from Caphtor and the Arameans from Kir" (Amos 9:7). Surely righteousness is more dear in God's eyes than any affiliation. Prior to the question of how glorious is our team should be the question of how worthy are our deeds and our hearts.

The Real Me

DO YOU HAVE A SOLID SELF? Identity is partly a personal construction: We build our selves from bits of other people. We take this one's interest in sports, another's way of dressing, a third's love for animals. In time they become our own. How much of that is really me? Is there a real me?

The Kotzker rebbe told his disciples, "If I am I because you are you and you are you because I am I, then I am not I, and you are not you. But if I am I because I am I and you are you because you are you, then I am I, and you are you." This stands as the quintessential definition of what is now fashionably known as codependence: If your identity is entirely dependent on others, then it is not really yours.

God identifies himself to Moses at the burning bush as "I am that I am." Human beings can never be so self-assured—or so self-defined. We constantly measure ourselves, pruning or expanding our characters in the light of others. But the Kotzker reminds us that fidelity to oneself is an important measure of integrity. As unique images of God, we honor God by becoming what in our uniqueness we were intended to be.

Music Others Cannot Hear

LUDWIG WITTGENSTEIN, perhaps the premier philosopher of the twentieth century, led a difficult and often tortured life. In his biography of Wittgenstein, *The Duty of Genius,* Ray Monk quotes the philosopher explaining to his disapproving sister why despite his fabulous talents, he decided to become a teacher in a rural school: "You remind me of somebody who is looking out through a closed window and cannot explain to himself the strange movements of a passerby. He cannot tell what sort of storm is raging out there and that this person might only be managing with difficulty to stay on his feet."

The Ba'al Shem Tov once used a similar image to explain how people sway and express love in prayer, moving to music others cannot hear. Whether in prayer or in the motions of life, we often find that the elements strike each of us in ways that differ more radically than others can possibly imagine. We move through life contending with obstacles or dancing to music that to others seems nonexistent.

No two people are exactly alike, nor are two struggles exactly alike. Both the philosopher and the rabbi point out that one cannot always feel one's way into another's soul. We can but trust and seek to help others along their individual journeys.

Do We Afflict Ourselves?

HOW MUCH OF OUR PAIN is self-inflicted? How much of our confusion is our own doing? As George Berkeley remarks, "We have first raised a dust and then complain we cannot see."

The midrash offers a kindred insight. The Rabbis tell us that when iron was created the trees began to tremble, for in the ax was their certain foe. God said to them, "Why are you trembling? If wood is not joined to it, not one of you will suffer." Without the ax handle, the iron is useless. The midrashic lesson is clear: That which we fear often gains its power through our own contribution.

In the Bible we see characters sabotaged by situations of their own creation. Saul's failings lead to David's rise, which then drives Saul deeper into despair. Jacob's favoring Joseph inflames the brothers' resentment, which for decades deprives Jacob of his beloved son.

Many of the ills that afflict us are a product of our creation or our consent. In his journal, Emerson writes, "Henry [Thoreau] made last night the fine remark that 'as long as a man stands in his own way, everything seems to be in his way.'" It has been that way since creation. Just ask the trees.

Our Own Prisons

RABBI ARYEH LEVIN was called the Holy Man of Jerusalem. He spent his adult life in Israel, where he visited prisoners, bringing them comfort, food, spiritual sustenance. Once after Passover some of the Jewish prisoners told Rabbi Aryeh that although the seder had been good, something important was missing: Because they were in prison, they could not perform the traditional rite of opening the door for Elijah, an act that invites redemption, for Elijah is the herald of the Messiah. Surely there was no enslavement more absolute than the inability to coax forth redemption.

Rabbi Aryeh replied, "Every man is in a prison of his own self. He cannot leave by going out of the house but only by passing through the door of the heart. And to make an opening for himself in his own heart—that anyone can do, even a prisoner behind bars. And then he will be in true spiritual freedom."

At each significant moment during the year, each of us should seek to understand where we are enslaved and open the door to our heart. That door is the portal of goodness, repentance, and faith.

Hidden in a Half-Shekel

THE BIBLE INSTRUCTS EACH ISRAELITE to pay a half-shekel as a census tax to the Temple (Exodus 30:13). The conventional explanation is that this amount permits every man, no matter what his means, to pay the tax. But the commentators had many other ideas as well.

Why a half-shekel? According to Rabbi Samson Rafael Hirsch, a half is a reminder of incompleteness. Even the most intense human effort is never complete; thus the half-shekel reminds us of the provisional nature of all our work in this world.

The half-shekel is, we are told, a *kofer nafsho*, a "redemption for one's soul." As Rabbi Milton Steinberg wrote so beautifully many years ago, every human being owes a debt to life. We redeem our souls because life is an unearned gift. We did not earn the sunlight and the stars, the air, the mountains, and seas. We should not feel guilty about this blessing, but we should feel responsible for it.

A half-shekel because, according to some commentators, each person should see himself or herself as half-redeemed in this world. The other half depends on how we live. Each moment could be decisive.

Finally, a half-shekel because it takes another to make us whole. We are all unfinished; we all seek completeness.

So much is hidden in a simple half-shekel.

Heroic Tears

IN THE BIBLE, Jacob cries, Rachel cries, Joseph cries, David cries. Through Isaiah, God says to King Hezekiah, "I have seen your tears" (Isaiah 38:5). In a midrash, God even criticizes the prophet Jeremiah because in the face of tragedy, Jeremiah does not cry.

Tears are the leitmotif of a people that has seen more than its share of pain. The Jewish people well understand why the poet Dante makes the inability to shed tears one of the tortures of the damned: Dante writes that in the bottommost pit in Hell, it is so cold that tears freeze on the cheeks of those who long to cry. In Judaism to cry and to cry out can be the only responses to a world that so often seems madly out of control.

Indeed, in the legends of the Rabbis, God cries as well. God cries over the depredations of human beings and over the afflictions of the Jewish people. Yes, Jewish heroes do cry; perhaps crying is even a requirement. Still, we cherish the hope that, as the psalmist writes, "Those who sow in tears shall reap in joy" (Psalm 126:5).

Renew the Old
and Sanctify the New

❦

WHAT IS OUR TASK for each new year in a world filled with rapid, dizzying change? Rabbi Israel Leventhal used to delight in the following midrash: In Deuteronomy we are told, "Remember the days of old; consider the years of many generations." The Gaon of Vilna was said to have read the Hebrew word *shanot* not as "years" but as "changes"—that is, "Consider the changes of various generations."

Each generation of human beings will change the world. If it does not, all the marvelous faculties with which we are endowed by God will be wasted. Preservation is a sacred task, but it is not our only task. We are bidden to sustain and to create.

Medical advances, scholarship, and knowledge increase exponentially. There are more changes now in a decade than there used to be in a millennium. We are caught up in Henry Adams's law of acceleration, with no sign of stopping.

Increasingly we understand the wisdom of Rav Kook's dictum: We are to renew the old and sanctify the new. As we contemplate the blizzard of innovations in our time, let us calmly consider the changes in our generation and resist the impulse to either embrace them all or reject them all just because they are new. Rather, we must measure modernity with the yardstick of ancient wisdom so that we might change as fruitfully and as reverently as did our ancestors.

∾

Struggling and Spirit

SPIRITUAL STATURE is the product of struggle. One is not born exalted. Too often we tell our children stories of heroes and neglect to remind them of the effort, the stumbling, the weariness, the doubt that lay along the path.

Rabbi Yitzḥak Hutner once observed that when we study the lives of spiritual giants, we concentrate on the end of the story. We do not hear about the years of struggling and stumbling. This renowned scholar and head of a yeshivah went on to write:

> As a result, when a young man who is imbued with spirit and ambition experiences impediments and downfalls, he believes that he is not planted in the house of God... However, know...that the key for your soul is not the tranquillity of *hayatzer hatov* [the good inclination] but the war against *hayatzer hara* [the evil inclination]. You have surely stumbled and will again, and you will be vanquished in many battles. However, I promise that after your losses, you will emerge with the victor's wreath on your head.

This moving letter was signed, "Sharing in your suffering, confident that you will prevail, praying for your success, Yitzḥak Hutner."

No one achieves perfection. Yet when we hear from those who have reached high stature that they, too, endured crisis and conflict, we may more easily put our own obstacles into pespective.

Understanding Life
Backward

⌒

HOW DO WE MAKE A PATTERN out of the disparate, multicolored threads of our lives? How do we construct our story from all the events and incidents that happen to us in our years on earth?

One function of faith is to help us shape the significant events of life. Holidays mark the rhythm of the season; life-cycle events mark the rhythm of the years; the patterns of the past are established by the rhythms of history. "The deeds of our ancestors presage the lives of their descendants," writes Naḥmanides. Tradition provides ways to arrange and understand our lives, which can often be understood through the struggles and successes of our predecessors. Gradually we watch as out of our own deeds a design emerges.

Kierkegaard writes that life must be lived forward but can only be understood backward. To put the insight differently, we might recall the poignant words of Rabbi Abraham Joshua Heschel, who writes that God speaks slowly in our lives, a syllable at a time; not until we reach the end of life can we read the sentences backward. Judaism offers us a way to understand God's words in our lives so that they are meaningful, even eloquent.

∿

What Should We Do with Lives That Are Limited?

OUR WORLD REFLECTS but a fraction of the possibilities of God's creativity. There is a rabbinic teaching that God created and destroyed many worlds before creating the one we know.

The philosopher Arthur Lovejoy identifies in the writings of Plato what he calls the principle of plentitude: that the world has or will contain the full diversity of living things. Nothing that could be will not be; there is no unrealized potential in the pageant of present and future life. But the midrash offers a contrary view: There is much we shall never see. There are possibilities—some beautiful and some brutal—that will forever remain unrealized.

Reducing such cosmic happenings to a human scale, we are left with the lesson of limitation: Too often we live as if all that can be will be. We do not believe that life is limited, that choices mean discarding that which is less important. We watch television hour after hour as though we would live forever; we bicker with our beloved over inanities as though sickness and death will never cut short the conversation; we act as if the world were governed by plentitude when in fact it is governed by limitation.

Worlds were sacrificed to make possible this rich, intense, brief life. Live now, while the world remains alive for you.

$\sim$

Are We Naturally Good?

∽

ARE WE NATURALLY GOOD? Some modern thinkers, following Rousseau, argue for the natural goodness of human beings. The classical Christian doctrine of original sin argues for the innate evil of human beings. There is enough kindness and surely enough evil in this world to support either notion. What does Judaism believe?

Judaism argues for neither proposition. People are neither naturally good nor naturally evil—they are naturally split. Each of us bears an inclination to good (*yatzer hatov*) and an inclination to evil (*yatzer hara*). Ecclesiastes asserts, "For there is no righteous person on this earth that does good and sins not" (7:20). Evil exists within even the most placid, loving heart. Yet powerful impulses to act altruistically and drives to better ourselves morally are also genuine aspects of our riven nature.

We praise children when they are good because goodness is difficult and takes work. We condemn evil because we know that while it is inside us, it is also within our capacity to rise above it. In the Torah, God declares, "I set before you this day life and death...Choose life!" (Deuteronomy 30:19). The ability to choose and choosing rightly together constitute the design and destiny of God's creation.

∽

Stand Before God

⌁

"FOR GOD BROUGHT ABOUT THE VICTORY. Once Beowulf had struggled to his feet, the holy and omniscient ruler of the sky easily settled the issue in favor of the right."

What is striking about those lines from the renowned early medieval epic, *Beowulf,* is how they embody the idea that God helps Beowulf once the warrior struggles to his feet. Beowulf must initiate his own salvation. God responds to self-assertion.

That same idea is beautifully expressed one thousand years before *Beowulf* in God's message to the prophet Ezekiel. When he begins to prophesy, God says to him, "Son of man, stand on your feet that I may speak to you" (Ezekiel 2:1). God cannot speak to a prostrate Ezekiel, one who is not aware of his own attributes and worth. For Ezekiel to prophesy, he must rise to his full height as a human being.

Deep faith always involves an element of submission—rampant egos block relationships. But deep faith does not demand dissolution of the self. One can stand strong without conceit; one can learn both to stand and to bow.

∿

Animal Instincts

❧∿☙

THE OMER MARKS THE FIFTY DAYS spent traveling through the desert from Egypt to Sinai. It also marks the wave offering of the Temple on the second day of Passover. The wave offering was a measure of flour made from the first sheaves of reaped barley.

What is the significance of counting the omer? Isaac Herzog, the late chief rabbi of Israel, writes that barley is *ma'achal behema,* "food fit for beasts." It is animal food. Why, then, did we offer it up in the Temple? Could it not have been construed as an insult?

We know, Herzog continues, that human beings share many things with animals. From a certain perspective we are a link on the biological chain and nothing more. But from a Jewish perspective it is our task to rise above animality alone, the rule of instinct, and to realize our higher nature.

The Talmud teaches that the purpose of the mitzvot is to refine human beings. That which begins as an animal instinct can, through the guidance of Torah, be refined until it becomes an expression of the Divine. The barley offering, which begins as a food for animals, must be sifted and refined, and then it may be offered to God. The omer represents the aspiration to ennoble instinct. We are animals, but we are not only animals. Sifted and refined, we are worthy of approaching God.

∿

Should We Flatter God?

WHY DO WE ASK GOD for things when we pray? Do we imagine that if we did not ask, God would not know what we desired? Do we suppose that an all-knowing God had not intended to grant us a certain gift, but on seeing our earnestness, on seeing how deeply we pray, God chooses to act otherwise? Is God simply flattered by the effusion of praise?

An analogy used by Leon of Modena explains: Imagine a man sitting in his boat on a lake, pulling himself, by means of a rope, back to shore. To someone standing far off, it might appear that he is moving the shore closer, but of course it is only the boat that moves. Similarly, Leon explains, people think they are moving God when they are in fact moving themselves. We are the boats, and God is the shore.

God does not need our flattery, but we need reminders of God's greatness. God does not change in response to our prayers, but we do. God remains unfathomable, but with each earnest prayer we come to understand ourselves better. With each pull, we draw closer to God. And if our prayer draws us closer to God, then the prayer has been answered.

A Room With Windows

THE TALMUD TEACHES that one should not pray in a room without windows. According to Rav Kook, this is because prayer without a recognition of the outside world—one's responsibilities and duties—is empty. Why should one choose to pray to God in a cramped, narrow corner, a place unrelated to the vast panorama of God's world?

The Talmud may also be making the reverse point: not that we look out, but that others must look in. To see someone lift a heart to God can itself be heartening. Knowing that devotion exists can kindle our devotion. Although we cannot be sure what goes on in another's heart (as Elizabeth I famously commented in her declaration of religious tolerance, "I seek not to carve windows into men's souls"), we can watch others pray and be inspired by the sight.

The Ba'al Shem Tov taught that when you see someone sway in prayer, you should not think it strange. Compare it to a man passing by a glass house inside which people are dancing: Since he cannot hear the music, he sees only the rhythms. The music may be playing even if we cannot hear it. How can we know? By looking through the windows.

VIRTUES AND VICES

෴

How can you expect me to be perfect...
when I am full of contradictions?

~ Moses Ibn Ezra

Ambition and Goodness

"THE JEALOUSY OF SCHOLARS advances learning," the Talmud tells us. We know that ambition and even envy can be productive. Our economic system is built on the beneficial effects of competition.

But there is a flip side:

Ambition breeds resentment. "It is not enough to succeed," says the mordant aphorist La Rochefoucauld; "one's friends must fail." Or to put it more simply, in the words of Ibn Gabirol, "Ambition is bondage." We begin by hoping to succeed. Soon we are in thrall to success.

How do we ensure that ambition serves sanctity? Judaism teaches that the aim of one's ambition is crucial. Do we struggle to better the world or to garner glory? Are we building the Tabernacle or the tower of Babel?

"The problem with the rat race," says Lily Tomlin, "is even if you win, you're still a rat." If we are spinning in the wheel of self-interest, that is true. But as the Talmud advises, if our ambition and even our envy are for learning, for goodness, for sanctity, for God, then ambition can be ennobled. If we ask ourselves what we are striving for, we are taking the first steps toward ensuring that our striving is worthy.

An Address for Gratitude

ONCE TWO BOOKS FROM DIFFERENT SOURCES landed on my desk on the same afternoon. One was a series of meditations by a rabbi, another a series of meditations by a philosopher who describes himself as a humanist. Both are full of wisdom about living one's life. But there is a glaring omission in the philosopher's work, a subject that is prominent in the rabbi's book: the chapter on gratitude.

Gratitude is more powerful if it has an address. For the rabbi, Judaism has made clear that gratitude is due to God. The first words spoken in prayer in the morning are *modeh ani*, "I am grateful to You, O God." When we repeat the Amidah, the hazan, the cantor, can recite every blessing on our behalf, but when it comes to Modim, the prayer of thanks, each congregant must recite it individually.

There is even a rabbinic opinion that in messianic times all the sacrifices will be abolished—except the thanksgiving sacrifice. For one thing that must never disappear is gratitude to God.

Despite our swagger we have received far more than we can possible give back. As Mark Twain quips, "The self-made man is no more likely than the self-laid egg." In a world without God, there is no address for our appreciation.

We who are daily showered with blessing must not ignore the centrality of gratitude. To give thanks softens our hearts, reminds us that we are but part of a greater whole, and directs us to God.

Showing Up

THE FREQUENCY WITH WHICH WE LIVE in states of inattention to our own lives is suggested by the ever proliferating means of distraction. We can avoid both conversation and introspection in this age of the Internet, television, MP3, DVD, and increasingly sophisticated portable message systems. We can be constantly in touch without ever being in contact.

The technology is new, but the syndrome is not. Among Nathaniel Hawthorne's random ideas for stories was an entry that read, "Suggestion for a story in which the principle character never appears."

To appreciate God's world is to fight against the lethargy of inattentiveness. A sense of blessing requires a sense of alertness to the wonder of creation. The morning blessings that thank God for the world, for the functions of our bodies, for the community of others, should (if recited properly) sharpen our sense of awareness.

The Swiss writer Max Frisch writes that technology is the knack of arranging the world so we do not have to experience it. It is easy to apply the same insulation to our souls that we do to our homes.

But emotional automation is soul death. To live with awareness is not egotism but appreciation. Life is not long, but it is much longer if it is lived.

Be Sure to Fail

❧

THE VERY WORD STICKS PINS in our hearts: *failure*. Yet what path to accomplishment is not strewn with the husks of failed efforts?

Indeed, the Talmud (Gitlin, 43a) teaches that "no one can truly understand Torah unless he has failed in it." The easy glide of success does not teach the deepest lessons. Nothing resembles a hollow so much as a swelling, and only one who knows failure will understand success. To overcome failure is the yardstick of attainment; to fear it is the guarantor of lethargy.

Unless we risk and unless we fail, we do not understand the depths of experience. When we set our internal standards and fall short, we begin to grow. The next time, our achievements and our standards are pushed to a higher rung.

Failure is not pleasant; it is, however, necessary. In the *midrash*, Rabbi Johanan teaches, "The eye has a white part and a dark part, but we can see only through the dark part." Through failure we can begin to see. From darkness comes insight. Given time and faith, insight brings triumph.

∿

Winning and Losing
at the Same Time

HERE IS A FAMOUS TEACHING from the *Pirkei Avot* (2:1). Do you see anything strange about the structure of the statement? "Measure the loss of the mitzvah against reward and the reward of a sin against its loss." As my teacher Rabbi Simon Greenberg once pointed out, the structure is chiastic: The first phrase, about a mitzvah, mentions the loss first; the second, about sin, mentions the reward first. Why?

His answer is that every mitzvah indeed begins with a loss: a loss of money, or of time, or of some other kind. And every sin begins with a gain—otherwise, why would one commit the sin? There is always a gain: of money, or pleasure, or something. So in deciding what action to perform, we must reckon the immediate consequence, gain or loss, against the eventual consequence, loss or gain.

Successful living depends in part on the maturity to take the long view. What thrills us now may be a temporary gain weighed against a deeper loss. What feels like a painful loss might, with the settled perspective of time, prove to be a marvelous gain.

Tactful Lying?

❧

ARE WE ALLOWED TO LIE? The Bible tells us to "stay far from falsehood" (Exodus 23:7). But the Talmud records an argument between the schools of Hillel and Shammai concerning whether one should praise a bride as beautiful if she is, well, less than beautiful. The school of Shammai says no and that of Hillel says yes, but the Hillelites try to escape the contradiction by insisting that on her wedding day, every bride is beautiful.

In the Bible, God misquotes Sarah's words to Abraham, tactfully leaving out Sarah's claim that her husband is too old to have a child (Genesis 18:12–13). The value of *sh'lom bayit*, "domestic harmony," overrides the value of honest reporting. Similarly, the Rabbis tell approvingly of Aaron's willingness to dissemble in order to ensure peace between friends who quarrel.

God's seal, teaches the *midrash*, is truth. But peace and decency are also cherished values. Weighing tenderness and honesty in the mix is not easy. We should watch our tongues and be aware of what we are doing and why. Or we can combine the advice of Hillel and Shammai, following the example of Jean Cocteau, the French artist who in declining a dinner invitation, sent a telegram reading, "Regret cannot come. Lie to follow."

～

Knowing What We Want

GETTING WHAT YOU WANT is hard enough, but how do you know what you want? As Stephen Sondheim puts it in *Into the Woods,* "How can you know what you want till you get what you want and you see if you like it?"

Part of the aim of prayer is to refine desire. Each day we are instructed to ask for certain things: We pray for the ingathering of the Jews, for the restoration of Israel, for health, for our own goodness, for an end to suffering, for peace. Do we always feel an active desire in us for all of those things? No. But the tradition recognizes that desires can lodge deep within. The wishes of the moment often override the more enduring yearning of the soul.

Gradually, through asking, the deep worthiness of those goals emerges. Years of asking for something helps crystallize its importance. Learning each day to long for something beyond ourselves expands our boundaries, allowing us to embrace others. We begin to want the kinds of things that at first we merely wished we wanted.

Judaism is not only a training in getting; it is also a training in wishing.

Turning to Face Each Other

❧

ON EITHER SIDE OF THE ARK IN THE TEMPLE were two k'ruvim, delicately carved golden angels. In the Book of Exodus (25:20), we are told that they faced each other. In the Book of 2 Chronicles (3:13), it is recorded that they were turned away from each other.

No gestures are more powerful than turning toward and turning away. There are times in our lives when we face another and times when we turn aside. The k'ruvim symbolized periods of intimacy with God and periods of distance. At the heart of the Temple was a reminder that closeness alternates with detachment.

We should not underestimate the power of movement. A lifetime of distance can be remedied by turning toward another. Conversely, even the deepest love can be damaged by turning away.

One translation of Psalm 103:12 is "As far as east is from west have our sins distanced us from God." "How far is east from west?" asks the Kotzker rebbe. At first it seems it is a whole world away. But if you face west, you need only turn around. T'shuvah, "repentance," is turning until, like the k'ruvim in the Ark, we face each other.

〜

You Shall Not Covet

IT IS OFTEN SAID THAT JUDAISM prescribes action, not emotion. To be sure, Jewish teaching does reckon with the quality of our thoughts and the range of our emotional life. Nonetheless, there is truth to the generality; we are a tradition exquisitely attuned to practice, to conduct, to law.

Think of our most famous set of laws, the Ten Commandments. Clearly they emphasize action. Yet suddenly at the end is the commandment "Do not covet." We understand that coveting can be powerfully destructive. But is it possible not to want what another has? And even if it is possible, can the tradition legislate our feelings?

Many explanations seek to unravel this conundrum. One of the most beautiful is the idea that all the previous commandments are intended to fulfill the last one: One who lives by God's word will feel successful and satisfied and so will not covet. We do not seek when we are content. Perhaps when the Torah enjoins, "You shall not covet," it is not a commandment but a promise.

∾

Religion in the Marketplace

❧⁓

WHAT COUNTS MORE, keeping kosher or running an honest business?

Traditionally we are taught that we should not weigh mitzvot, comparing one to the other. Yet it might surprise many Jews to know that, as the Israeli banker and scholar Meir Tamari points out, the Torah has twenty-four regulations about kashrut and over one hundred about economic justice.

How important is it to be honest in business? When an individual comes before God, the Talmud teaches, he or she will be asked a series of questions. The very first question is "Were you honest in your business dealings?" (*Shabbat* 31a).

Judaism is not a faith confined to the home or the synagogue; its mission is to bring a sense of sanctity into all areas of life. When the psalmist writes, "I will walk before God in the land of the living" (Psalms 116:9), the Rabbis add that "the living" refers to the marketplace (*Yoma* 71a). In buying and selling, in browsing and bargaining through these daily activities, our true character is often revealed.

"If one is honest in business and earns the esteem of others, it is as if one has fulfilled the whole Torah" (*Mekhilta, Vayassa*). Religion may begin at home, but it should never end there.

⁓

The Virtues of Inaction

THERE ARE MITZVOT THAT ARE POSITIVE—active mitzvot—and mitzvot that are called negative. The negative mitzvot involve not doing something—not stealing, not bearing false witness.

Often what does not happen makes the deepest impression on us. Readers of Sherlock Holmes remember the dog that does not bark in the night. Readers of the Bible are startled by the bush that is not consumed.

People, too, amaze us not only with their reactions but also with their ability to refrain from reacting. Abraham Lincoln avoided the bitterness one might have expected in the wake of a civil war. The same lack of resentment was glowingly apparent in Nelson Mandela's demeanor after his release from prison. In the Torah we read of Moses's tranquillity in the face of others who prophesied among the people. Rather than showing jealousy or anger, Moses takes the news calmly, simply wishing that more of God's children would be prophets.

Judaism is a religion not only of action but also of artful inaction. It teaches us hishtalvut, "equanimity," a quality that enables us to know when by not acting we can make the most profound statement.

What Is So Wrong
with Idolatry?

WHY ARE IDOLS PROHIBITED? Most think it is because God has no image and therefore to fashion an image of God is sacrilege. But in his book, *Seek My Face, Speak My Name*, Arthur Green brings us a beautiful teaching of Rabbi Abraham Joshua Heschel's that explains idolatry differently.

Idols are forbidden, says Heschel, because there exists an image of God; it is found in every human being. Therefore, there is only one medium in which one may fashion an image of God, and that is the medium of one's life. The message of the Torah is to make oneself a worthy image of God and not seek images of God in the idols that we create with our own hands.

As images of God, we are given a sacred task: to reflect that divine image in our lives each day. A mitzvah is a brushstroke; a well-lived life is a portrait composed of goodness and meaning. Given the great privilege of creating art from our lives, we are not permitted to worship that which we fashion with our own hands; we may worship only that which is reflected through a good life: the presence of God.

Digging Up the Hatchet

﹏

ACCORDING TO ONE RABBINIC TEACHING, Rosh Hashanah celebrates the day human beings were created. That sixth day of creation is the day on which Adam and Eve were placed in the garden, ate the fruit, were ejected from the garden, and were forgiven by God.

The point of this tradition is that the world begins with forgiveness. Yes, there is sin in the beginning as well, but it is the emphasis on forgiveness that distinguishes the teaching and preoccupies the Rabbis. For as we learn in another midrash, without the quality of mercy the world cannot endure.

Forgiveness is far easier in theory than in practice. The humorist Kin Hubbard wrote that "nobody ever forgets where he buried the hatchet." We sometimes believe we forgive, but the original insult rankles; we are often incomplete in our mercy. We nurture the grudge as we exalt the absolution.

In the Bible the human journey begins with sin and forgiveness. One is natural, the other necessary. Every one of us will sin, but will we forgive?

﹏

Earnings or Gifts?

ACCORDING TO THE TORAH, each Israelite was asked to contribute a half-shekel to the Temple (Exodus 30:12). The Hebrew for "and you shall give" is v'natnu. V'natnu is a palindrome: It can be read the same way forward and backward. The Vilna Gaon comments that this is to remind us that one who gives today may need to receive tomorrow.

It is easy to confuse good luck with earned rewards. Many who are fortunate consider not their fortune but their merit. "Of course I have done well," goes the self-satisfied refrain; "I worked hard." That may be true, but many work hard and fail. Still others work, or have worked, hard in environments, countries, professions, and ages when hard work is not rewarded. Many are not born with endowments that enable them to flourish, even with great effort.

Most of what we have in this life is a gift, and gifts are not permanent. Therefore, we are enjoined by our tradition to give to others not out of a largeness of heart—although that, too, is important—but out of simple justice. As the Vilna Gaon reminds us, our good fortune is not an earned payment but a bounty of God. Ultimately, God's benefactions belong to all.

The Gift of Friendship

IS THERE A BLESSING GREATER than good friends? "Either friends or death," ringingly declares the Talmud (Ta'anit, 23a). The sages insist that isolation is a betrayal of God's design. People need one another to thrive.

The Bible is a book of deep friendships: Jonathan and David's, Ruth and Naomi's. Each illustrates the depth of true friendship, which involves not only love but also the willingness of one to make sacrifices for the interests of the other. True friendship is not selfish and does not disappear when the friend is in trouble. Who does not understand the pathos of false friends as expressed by the world featherweight champion Willie Pep, describing what happens to a boxer as he grows old: "First your legs go. Then you lose your reflexes. Then you lose your friends."

Real friends don't leave.

Deep friendship is mysterious. It is not always based on a community of interests or a congruence of goals. Groping for a means of expressing his famous friendship with Étienne de La Boétie, Montaigne writes, "If you press me to tell why I loved him, I feel that this cannot be expressed, except by answering: Because it was he, because it was I."

Among the glorious gifts celebrated by our tradition is this peculiar and lasting love, the friend.

~

The Most Important
Thing in Life

∾

RABBI ISRAEL SALANTER, founder of the Musar movement, which emphasized decency, civility, and kindness in addition to Talmudic scholarship. He recognized that ritual observance was not enough: It must be built on a foundation of benevolence.

Many stories are told of Rabbi Salanter's goodness. Once before a meal, he saw the other diners performing the ritual washing with copious amounts of water. He used just a sprinkling. When asked why, he answered, "Because you are concerned for your own mitzvah. I am concerned about the serving woman who has to trudge out in the cold to bring your water from the well." Rabbi Israel taught that we should first be concerned with our own souls and others' bodies rather than always being concerned about our own bodies and others' souls.

Rabbi Israel told his disciples once that it is easy to declare God Sovereign of the Universe. It is difficult to declare God sovereign over oneself. The rabbi knew how easily rationalization and indifference can defeat our best efforts. His teaching gives Jewish shape to the advice of the great writer Henry James: "Three things in human life are important; the first is to be kind; the second is to be kind; and the third is to be kind."

∾

Finding the Key

THE RABBIS TELL THE STORY of the High Priest who, as the Temple was being consumed in flames, hurled the keys heavenward and watched the figure of a hand emerge from the sky to receive them.

David Roskies's book *Against the Apocalypse* begins by recounting the tale of Moroccan Jews who are said to retain the keys to their ancestral homes in Spain and Portugal.

God, we are told in the *midrash*, holds three keys: to the womb (fertility), to rain, and to resurrection.

Once, lecturing in Texas, I met a man who had run a convenience store with his wife for twenty-five years. When she died and he had to shut up the store, he could find no key, for the door had never been closed.

The novelist John Barth writes in the short story "Dunyazadiad," "The key to the treasure is the treasure."

Keys and locks, real and metaphorical, meet us at every crosswalk of life. Like the man in Kafka's parable, some people waste their lives standing before a door that will never open for them. Part of the artistry of life is knowing which locks we really do wish to open and to which locks we already possess the key.

The Art of Goodness

IN HIS BOOK, THE MORAL SENSE, the sociologist James Q. Wilson writes, "The forces that may easily drive people to break the law—a desire for food, sex, wealth, and self-preservation—seem to be instinctive, not learned, while those that restrain our appetites—self-control, sympathy, a sense of fairness—seem to be learned and not instinctive."

In other words we need to train ourselves not to want but to refrain. Often the great drive in life is portrayed as the drive to liberate need, to recognize, refine, and realize desire. Subject to a fluctuating reputation over time, Dionysius is getting pretty good press these days.

But the truly difficult challenge of life, the one on which our continued survival depends, is not the liberation of need but its proper channeling. Seneca said it long ago: "Nature does not bestow virtue; to be good is an art." Or as the Rabbis put it, "Everything is in the hands of heaven except the fear of heaven."

We are granted a range of desires and a world full of good with which to satisfy them. That is our endowment. To use them for good is our task.

Insight at Quiet Times

✥

IN HIS BOOK, *DARWIN'S DANGEROUS IDEA*, the scientist and philosopher Daniel Dennett writes about the principle of quiescence in chess. A good chess player will always look a few moves beyond any flurry of exchanges to see what the board will look like when it quiets down. Dennett asserts that there is no similar principle in life. Life is always in flux, he says, and there is no still moment that defines an endpoint to evaluate what is likely to be in the future. But in interpersonal life there are moments of quiescence. Young couples, preparing to be married, go through the stresses of planning a wedding, imagining a life together, getting accustomed to each other's families. Those events can appear all-consuming; it seems that the wedding will always dominate their lives. Wise couples seek to look beyond the moment to the quiescence that follows and to consider what life will be like when the wedding is behind them, when the families are more familiar, when routine has replaced the first frisson of romance.

Life often demands important decisions at tumultuous times. But as the *Talmud* (Tamid, 32a) teaches us, "Who is wise? *Haro'eh et hanolad*, 'one who can envision what he brings into being.'" There is a quiet point inside ourselves where we can, by dint of reflection and detachment, come to see the shape assumed by our lives after the decision has been made. Through such clarity we take responsibility for our lives and seek to make them holy.

∿

Tying Love and Hate Together

⌒∿⌒

IN HIS ESSAY, "The French as Dostoevsky Saw Them," Saul Bellow writes, "It does not surprise modern readers, acquainted with twentieth-century psychology, that the power to hate increases the power to love also. The duc de Saint-Simon said long ago that love and hate were fed by a single nerve. The same thought is expressed clearly enough by William Blake, and Dostoevsky was not ignorant of it."

Let us push the pedigree back a bit. More than a millennium before Saint-Simon, a midrash offers the same insight. Commenting on the fact that Abraham, out of love, saddles his donkey early to perform the akedah, the binding of Isaac, and Bilam, the sorcerer, saddles his donkey early to (putatively) curse Israel, the midrash notes that each of those men would normally have had servants perform this menial task. But since acts of love and hate are so intensely personal, they wished to do it themselves. The rabbinic conclusion? "Both love and hate disturb the usual patterns of living" (Genesis Rabbah 55:8). These passions resemble each other in uncomfortable ways. They even feed each other, as Bilam's talent for cursing feeds the poetry of his blessing.

Bellow is certainly correct; any reader of modern psychology would understand. But then so would any student of the Bible who reads through the eyes of the Rabbis.

∿

Deliberation and Daring

⌣

WHEN THE ISRAELITES came to the Red Sea, it did not part. Even Moses's entreaties to God could not get the sea to split. The Rabbis recount that one man, Naḥshon ben Aminadav, boldly leapt into the sea, and then it parted. Like Curtius who flung himself into the breach in the floor of the Roman Senate, Naḥshon proved that what mattered was the courage to act when others falter.

There are always good reasons to hesitate. Considerations of prudence, of fairness, of deference, encourage us to hold back. Psychologists tell us that the greater the number of people who might respond, the less likely it is that any individual will take responsibility. So why did Naḥshon leap into the sea while all of Israel stood at the bank? Because he knew that at decisive moments in history, to hope, to dream, even to pray, is not enough. Deliberation is eclipsed by daring.

Herzl once told some friends, "I am not better nor more clever than any of you. But I remain undaunted, and that is why the leadership belongs to me." Among the children of Israel there were good people, wise people, even faithful people who cried out to God. But Naḥshon jumped.

⌣

Selfish Genes

WE LIVE IN AN AGE in which behavior is often explained anthropologically and evolutionarily. Evolutionary psychology explains the range of human conduct based on what we once were, primitives roaming the savannas. Our mating habits, the differences in male and female behavior, the jockeying for social position and power—all are subject to the often intriguing speculations of evolutionary biologists.

Perhaps the most famous example is the supposition that we are altruistic because we want to perpetuate our own genes—the selfish gene, as it was cleverly dubbed by Richard Dawkins: We will sacrifice ourselves if it means we perpetuate our genetic material. The renowned biologist J. B. S. Haldane once wittily answered when asked whether he wouldlay down his life for a brother, "For two brothers—or eight cousins."

But Judaism values acts performed in secret for the benefit of those we do not even know and from which we derive no social status. We are shaped by more than our genes; we are shaped by spirit. Contrary to what the evolutionary psychologists might say, giving tzedakah to one we do not know is a greater mitzvah than giving tzedakah to one who is able to thank us personally. "I have done one braver thing," writes the poet John Donne, "Than all the Worthies did;/ And yet a braver thence doth spring,/ Which is, to keep that hid."

Kindness to Strangers

MOST PEOPLE ARE COURTEOUS to those they barely know. We are gracious to the waiter, the elevator operator, the bank teller. But character is judged by how we behave when it is difficult to be kind. In other words, how do we behave to those who are close to us?

When two mitzvot are before us, one rare and the other commonplace, which takes priority? We might think the rare one. But there is a Jewish legal principle, *tadir usheino tadir, tadir kodem,* "the more frequently observed mitzvah takes precedence." It is not difficult to feel enthusiasm for the rare and special. The trick of life is to give the commonplace its due intensity.

The same principle should govern our relationships with people. Our first obligation of goodness, of courtesy, is to our spouses, our children, our family, our friends. Taking them for granted violates the principle of *tadir kodem,* the more frequent comes first.

A good life is marked in part by the stability of its relationships. Do we give those close to us the attention we lavish on those who are tangential in our lives? Everyone honors the special. Judaism teaches us to honor the everyday.

Thanks for Giving Thanks

HOW MANY BLESSINGS ARE SHOWERED ON US each day of our lives? We eat food we did not grow, use products we did not make, exercise natural talents we did not earn. The intelligent person takes pride in intelligence, the beautiful one in beauty, though both intelligence and beauty are gifts.

Judaism continually reminds us that gratitude is the proper disposition of a soul. One Talmudic teaching even proclaims that in messianic times, when the Temple is rebuilt, the only sacrificial offering will be the thanksgiving offering. For when the world is redeemed, we will demonstrate our worthiness by showing gratitude for the blessings we have been given.

Eugene Borowitz writes in *Renewing the Covenant*, "In my experience, what God gives most people hour by hour most generously exceeds what, as a simple matter of justice, they deserve. When one lives in gratitude, the absence of justice stands out primarily in the astonishing benevolence showered on most people."

In the Talmud (Sotah, 40a), Rav says, "We should give thanks to God each day that we areable to give thanks." Some stagger under great burdens of sadness. But for most of us, how can it be possible to be alive, feeling the plentitude of favors we have been given, and not be grateful?

Love and Law

❧

A CONFERENCE ORGANIZED BY ELIE WIESEL brought notable thinkers together from all over the world to respond to the questions "Why do people hate?" and "Why do people band together to express hatred?"

The group was distinguished, the speeches beautiful, and the resolutions firm. But as I learned from my colleague Rabbi Brad Artson, there was one notable conclusion, seemingly at odds with common sense. What can overcome hatred? "Only the belief in and execution of the law."

For the Jewish people that is not merely common sense but a commonplace. Ours is a tradition of law; we understand that mitzvot surround us in our lives. Judaism has long taught that a life embedded in law is a life of goodness, justice, purity.

Rabbi Arthur Hertzberg once pointed out that the Talmud begins and ends with a consideration of laws of purity. He interprets that as the Talmud's exhortation to "live always the life which passes moral muster, in which the differences between tumah (impurity) and taharah (purity) are defined in our daily behavior."

In a complex, interconnected world, the opposite of hate is not love but law. Purity and mitzvot seem increasingly not only the wisdom of the ages but an imperative of our age.

∼

LIFE, DEATH, AND AFTERLIFE

❧

Joy and sadness are as close as day and night.

~ Rabbi Chaim of Volozhin

Facing Death

WHAT DOES IT MEAN TO FACE DEATH? The Rabbis give us a hint from a subtle change in wording concerning the death of King David. Perhaps no character in the Bible is more vital than David: a warrior, a lover, a poet, a sinner, a savior of Israel. Now David is old and cannot even keep himself warm.

In the first verse of 1 Kings, we read, "Now King David was old." One chapter later his condition has declined: "Now the days of David drew near that he should die." Do you notice the difference?

In the first verse the hero of Israel is still King David. But as he faces death, he is simply David. The delicate difference contains a great teaching: Most of our lives, even in old age, we can hide behind position and power, behind titles and social forms. But all that melts away when we truly face our mortality. No one faces death as a king, or a rabbi, or a doctor, or a tycoon. We all face death as "David": as the simple sum of who we are. When we come to grips with our own finality, we stand exposed before God—and we learn the truth about ourselves.

When Does Real Life Start?

SCHOOLCHILDREN ARE OFTEN TOLD, "This is not real life." When students are in college, they are told, "This is not real life." Real life is something harsh, uncompromising, something that destroys illusions. It also lasts longer than college.

All of that is nonsense. Real life does not begin when you get out of college, or get married, or have children, or become a grandparent. It is not real only when painful or only when perfect. Such notions persuade people to wait all their lives for life to begin.

From Nabokov's novel, Pnin:

> A heated exchange between Professor Bolotov, who taught the history of philosophy, and Professor Chateau, who taught the philosophy of history: "Reality is Duration," one voice, Bolotov's, would boom. "It is not," the other would cry. "A soap bubble is as real as a fossil tooth."

There is suffering, growth, wisdom, and joy in short bursts of life in every setting. Enduring and evanescent are both real. Those who spend life anticipating the day they will *really* live will come to old age having squandered their one great, unrepeatable gift. In a world in which life is imperiled, the Torah insists, uvaḥarta baḥayim, "choose life." Choose it at every age, at every moment. It may be better or worse for you in the future than it is now, but it will never be more real.

Birthdays and Yarzheits

HISTORICALLY JEWS DID NOT PUT MUCH STOCK in birthdays. For most of our ancestors, birthdays were not a grand day to be marked and celebrated. But the date of death—that was not to be forgotten. A *yarzheit* (as the day came to be called in the Middle Ages) was a solemnly observed occasion.

In modern America we consider one's date of birth significant, but we tend to neglect the anniversary of a death. Perhaps the difference is attributable to Judaism's interest in evaluating the sum of a life, for a life cannot be assessed until its end. A birthday says only that one lives, not what one has accomplished. A *yarzheit* recalls not just the years but the content of the life.

Years ago my father told me that the saddest person in the Bible is Methuselah, because all the Bible tells us is that he lived 969 years and had children. Imagine—all those years and not one word about what he taught his children, not one accomplishment worth recording.

What matters is not when you come into this world but what you do while you are here.

While the Candle Burns

⁓

DESPITE THE PROLIFERATION OF THERAPIES, self-help gurus, and how-to books, changing one's life is an arduous business. We are not wired for upheaval; as the old therapeutic adage has it, we change only on the edge of anxiety, when the old internal systems have crashed and there is little choice.

So it is a statement of true faith that Judaism builds on the changeability of human beings. We are faithful to the possibility that a person can transform himself or herself not only by crisis but also by resolution. We hold that we can create a sort of crisis in the soul when we realize the brevity of life, the importance of the tasks we have been given, the power of love, and the majesty of the Divine. Much of Judaism is designed to help us to those realizations in the hope that we will turn them into change.

Rabbi Israel Salanter was once passing by the shop of a shoemaker and saw the man working late. He asked, "Why are you still working, the candle has almost gone out?" The shoemaker answered, "Rabbi, as long as the candle burns, one can still do some mending." That became Rabbi Salanter's motto: As long as the candle of our soul still burns, we should not despair of change.

⁓

~ *David J. Wolpe* ~

Are We Strangers
or Residents?

❦

ARE WE TRULY AT HOME IN THIS WORLD?

The Torah speaks about "strangers and residents" (Leviticus 25:23). How can one be both, a stranger and a resident? According to the maggid of Dubno, God is sending a signal about our proper attitude toward this world. If we feel too much at home, says the maggid, God will be a stranger to us. But if we feel a bit like strangers, God will be resident among us. The key is to understand that the world is a temporary home; we are renters, not owners.

Once a group of American visitors went to see the Ḥafetz Ḥaim. With great anticipation they were ushered into the famous rabbi's study. There they saw a small man sitting at a rickety desk on which sat a few books. In surprise one of the visitors blurted out, "Rabbi, where are all your possessions?" The Ḥafetz Ḥaim smiled and replied, "Where are all of yours?" The man answered, "We have very few possessions with us. After all, we are just passing through." The rabbi nodded and said, "Me too."

∿

The Losses of Life

WE RECITE YIZKOR FOR THOSE WHO HAVE DIED. But what of things that have died? Where is the *yizkor* for lost relationships, for dreams that have disappeared, for dimly remembered childhoods and homes and hopes? We live lifetimes of loss and do not know how to grieve.

For many people, faith begins in the assurance that life will not involve loss. Soon they discover that such faith is a chimera. There is no promise of a painless life. We can never know why the world is arranged so that loss is woven into the fabric of living. Faith that promises ease is false and unworthy.

Deep faith does promises not that we will never lose but that we can try to make the losses meaningful. Out of patterns of pain as well as joy and love, we create a moral work of art. At each moment, circumstance confronts us with the possibility of climbing the ladder of loss to reach higher than we were before.

We should resolve to take all of life—its tragedies as well as its gladness—and use it to make life more beautiful, more purposeful, more sacred.

What We Really Need to Live

WHAT DO WE NEED IN ORDER TO LIVE? Our first inclination is to name material objects: food, shelter, clothing. But other answers go deeper: Rabbi Hugo Gryn tells of being in a concentration camp in the winter of 1944:

> My father took me and some friends to a corner in the barracks. He announced that it was eve of Ḥanukkah and produced a small clay bowl. Then he began to light a wick immersed in his precious but now melted margarine ration. Before he could recite the blessing, I protested at this waste of food. He looked at me, then the lamp, and finally said, "You and I have seen that it is possible to live up to three weeks without food. We once lived almost three days without water. But you cannot live properly for three minutes without hope."

At times we hear a fashionable utterance of despair about the world, about human nature, about the future. Unthinkingly we pass such cynicism on to our children. But even in the darkest times the wisest among us understood that one cannot do without the essential ingredient of survival: hope.

Looking at Your Watch — Again

IN HIS HISTORY OF THE TWENTIETH CENTURY, Peter Conrad quotes Spengler, pointing out that we in the modern world are obsessive clock-watchers, mesmerized by that "dread symbol" of own mortal brevity. Through physics the Greeks studied a static world, but we are obsessed with dynamics and therefore so haunted by abbreviation that we compute time in thousandths of a second.

In *Gulliver's Travels*, Gulliver looks at his watch so often that his hosts, the Brobdingnagians, think he is consulting his god. Not only do we moderns fail to look at things under the aspect of eternity, but we can rarely stretch our vision past the next moment, so compulsively do we parcel out time.

On Sukkot we read Kohelet, which reminds us that there is a time for everything under the heavens. Our obsession with measuring that time will not slow it down or enable us to savor it more fully. I have never seen a clock hanging in a sukkah, for the sukkah itself is a symbol of impermanence. We do not need the sweep of the second hand when there is *schach* overhead.

When you enter the synagogue, leave your watch outside. On Shabbat evening, take a walk, and instead of counting the minutes, count the stars.

How to Think About Death

EVERYTHING THAT IS BORN DIES. We acknowledge our mortality, but should we give it much thought? The Spanish philosopher Miguel de Unamuno notes that "Socrates is a man; all men are mortal; therefore, Socrates is mortal"—a syllogism that used to be taught in logic classes—sounds very different when rendered "I am a man; all men are mortal; therefore, I will die."

Spinoza, architect of the most serene philosophy in the history of thought, writes in his Ethics that a wise man does not think about death. On the other hand, Freud, a far more turbulent savant, recalls the proverb "If you want to preserve peace, arm for war." He adds, "If you want to endure life, prepare for death."

Judaism demands that we pay attention to this world yet reminds us of our eventual fate. We are continually reminded that our lives are fleeting, like the wind that blows, like the flower that fades. Judaism asks us to grasp both ends in a paradoxical affirmation of faith: We know we will die, but that realization should not govern our lives. Rather, the knowledge of our mortality, always in the background, gives vividness and urgency to our days.

Deserving Eternity

DO WE LIVE FOREVER? The surge of popular supernatural-ism—everything from angels to out-of-body experiences—suggests a renewed interest in that question. Many Jews are unaware that Judaism has long maintained a firm belief in a life after death. *Olam Haba,* "the World to Come," is a staple of Jewish tradition, although exactly what that world is like is left tantalizingly vague.

Clouds of nonsense always accumulate around the unknown. Mark Twain writes that many believe that after death they will lie on green fields and listen to harp music—something they would not be happy doing for five minutes while alive but they imagine will contribute to their bliss for all eternity.

Miguel de Unamuno, the Spanish philosopher, writes in his *Tragic Sense of Life* that "no logical proof of immortality exists, but you should spend your life so that you deserve to be immortal." In other words, we do not know what happens after death, but we are in control of what happens in this life. If we manage to bring light to this world, perhaps one day we shall be privileged to peek over the horizon.

The Pony and the
Plain Pine Box

THE AVERAGE AMERICAN HOME is a few hundred square feet larger than it was two decades ago. Cars have grown into SUVs, corner markets have become mini-malls, television sets have evolved into small movie screens.

Nonetheless, huddled inside our plaster castles or stiff armed behind the wheel of our turret-free tank, we are the same frail, questioning creatures. Why do our possessions look as though we were feeding them steroids?

The child whose bar mitzvah celebration becomes a faux Roman gladiator spectacle (since one needs a theme) is still a child. But he has learned that the passage into Jewish adulthood is a road paved with ostentation and garishness. Is it any wonder that he moves swiftly along that road in later years?

"Things are in the saddle, writes Emerson, "and ride mankind." So the bat mitzvah rides in on a pony and her parents beam because they have shown the world not who they are but what they can afford.

But if we are important because of our things, we accord the image of God inside us no dignity.

Jewish tradition prescribes a plain pine box for burial. Everyone, peasant to potentate, should have the same coffin. Do not be deceived; your possessions do not fend off the ills of life. Rather, by keeping them in perspective, you enhance your life and honor God.

Funny Forever

~

WHO ATTAINS THE AFTERLIFE? Whatever redemption might be, the question of who can earn it preoccupies the Jewish tradition. It is another way of asking, What sort of life is considered exemplary in this world?

As we might expect, great scholars, sages, and those of exceptional piety are said repeatedly to inherit the world to come. But the Rabbis are always more interesting and nuanced than we might suppose. In the Talmud we read that a certain Rav Beroka once met Elijah the prophet in the marketplace. Visitations from Elijah are periodically recorded in rabbinic literature; Elijah brings wisdom and counsel to this world.

Rav Beroka asks who of those in the marketplace will inherit the world to come. Elijah points to two men.

"What is your occupation?" Rav Beroka asks them.

They answer, "We are jesters. We make the sad laugh, and when we see two people arguing, we try to make peace between them" (Ta'anit, 22a).

To bring joy to the world is noble. The sound of study is not necessarily holier than the music of laughter.

~

Aristocrats of the Imagination

❦

IN THE TALMUD (BABA BATHRA, 12B), Rabbi Johanan teaches that "from the day the Temple was destroyed, prophecy was taken from the prophets and given over to fools and to young children."

That remarkable statement has been the subject of many interpretations. Judaism is a tradition of learning and interpretation, law and lore. A continuation of prophecy threatens to overturn important ideas in the tradition: What if one can arise and say, "This is what God wants"? A declaration from one who hears a message directly from God threatens the tradition.

But given that caution, what is Rabbi Johanan's message? What do fools and young children have in common? It is precisely the irrationality of his statement that labels someone a fool. And young children are blissfully and splendidly unaware of the presumed limits of rationality. Fools and young children are aristocrats of the imagination.

So perhaps prophecy is tied to the ability to imagine the miraculous, the confounding, the impossible—and believe it can happen. The scientist and skeptic T.H. Huxley writes, "No conceivable event, however extraordinary, is impossible; and therefore, if by the term *miracles* we mean only 'extremely wonderful events,' there can be no just grounds for denying the possibility of their occurrence." Are miracles possible? When scientists, rabbis, fools, and young children speak with one voice, we should pay heed.

~

Can We Cheat the Prophet?

❧

I WAS ONCE ASKED TO SPEAK on the topic of Judaism in the twenty-first century. The invitation brought to mind the opening paragraph of G. K. Chesterton's novel *The Napoleon of Notting Hill*:

> The human race, to which so many of my readers belong, has been playing at children's games from the beginning... One of the games to which it is most attached is called... "Cheat the Prophet." The players listen very carefully and respectfully to all that the clever men have to say about what is to happen in the next generation. The players then wait until all the clever men are dead, and bury them nicely. They then go and do something else. That is all. For a race of simple tastes, however, it is great fun.

Anyone who listens to pundits and prognosticators knows that there are many more ways to be wrong than to be right. Each week and each year predictions are confidently offered, and then Chesterton's game begins, and we do something else. The only prediction of which we can be sure is that most of the predictions will be proved wrong. What will happen to Judaism in the twenty-first century? Something unpredictable, no doubt.

∿

A Life After This One

◦∼◦

IS THIS LIFE ALL?

The question of the afterlife has been debated throughout history. Although the Bible makes scant mention of the possibility (see Daniel 12), the Talmud is filled with the idea of *Olam Haba*, "the World to Come."

The classic Jewish compendium on the laws of death and mourning, *Gesher Ḥahayim* (*The Bridge of Life*), opens with an intriguing analogy. It asks the reader to imagine twins lying together in the womb. One of them believes "irrationally" that there is a world beyond the womb. The other is convinced such beliefs are nonsense. Suddenly the "believer" is forced through the birth canal. Imagine, asks the author, how the twin left behind must view this: A great catastrophe has just befallen the other. Outside the womb, however, the parents are rejoicing. For what the twin left behind has just witnessed is not death but birth.

Perhaps this is a gestational world. Could death be a birth? As the great Henry James wistfully said, it takes a whole life to learn how to live, "which is absurd if there's not another life in which to apply the lessons."

∼